THE GREENHAVEN PRESS

Literary Companion

TO AMERICAN LITERATURE

READINGS ON

THE PRINCE AND THE PAUPER

Jann Einfeld, *Book Editor*

Bonnie Szumski, *Series Editor*

Greenhaven Press, Inc., San Diego, CA

Every effort has been made to trace the owners of copy-righted material. The articles in this volume may have been edited for content, length, and/or reading level. The titles have been changed to enhance the editorial purpose. Those interested in locating the original source will find the complete citation on the first page of each article.

Library of Congress Cataloging-in-Publication Data

Readings on The prince and the pauper / Jann Einfeld,
    book editor.
        p. cm. — (The Greenhaven Press literary
    companion to American literature)
        Includes bibliographical references and index.
        ISBN 0-7377-0445-4 (pbk. : alk. paper). —
    ISBN 0-7377-0446-2 (lib. : alk. paper)
        1. Twain, Mark, 1835–1910. Prince and the pauper.
    2. Edward VI, King of England, 1537–1553—In literature.
    3. Historical fiction, American—History and criticism.
    4. Imposters and imposture in literature. 5. London
    (England)—In literature. 6. Princes in literature. 7. Boys
    in literature. 8. Poor in literature. I. Einfeld, Jann.
    II. Series.

PS1316.R43   2001
813'.4—dc21   00-068176
                                                      CIP

Copyright © 2001 by Greenhaven Press, Inc.
PO Box 289009
San Diego, CA 92198-9009
Printed in the U.S.A.

" You can find in a text whatever you bring, if you will stand between it and the mirror of your imagination. You may not see your ears, but they will be there. "

—Mark Twain, 1909

CONTENTS

Chapter 1: Origins and Context

1. How the Novel Came to Be Written
by Albert Bigelow Paine
Mark Twain's chosen biographer reports his discussions
with the author on the origins, purpose, plot, and his personal reaction to writing *The Prince and the Pauper.*

2. Nook Farm Writers and the Genteel Tradition
by Kenneth R. Andrews
The Prince and the Pauper was a product of the influence
of a genteel writing circle in Hartford, Connecticut, that
steered Mark Twain toward more serious and refined
writing. While claims by critics that this society stifled
Twain's spirit and emasculated his work are not true, it is
fair to say that the characters in *The Prince and the Pauper*
pale in comparison to those drawn directly from Twain's
life on the Mississippi River.

3. Documenting the Historical Sources
by Leon T. Dickinson
The practice of documenting the sources he used in writing his novel was related to Twain's belief, common
among Western writers of the day, that serious works of
fiction based on historical fact were superior to purely
imaginative works.

4. The Novel in Its Literary Context
by Marcus Cunliffe
Mark Twain was keen to establish an American claim to
the literary stature of authors like Charles Dickens and
William Thackeray. Despite modern preference for his
homegrown works, *The Prince and the Pauper* demonstrated both his versatility and superior command of the
historical romance, a genre fashionable in his day.

fate of humanity. The novel's emphasis on the moral decline of Tom Canty is evidence of Twain's internal struggle between hope and despair, his preoccupation with the fragility of human nature, and his underlying pessimism.

Chapter 4: The Issue of Identity

FOREWORD

*"'Tis the good reader that
makes the good book."*

Ralph Waldo Emerson

The story's bare facts are simple: The captain, an old and scarred seafarer, walks with a peg leg made of whale ivory. He relentlessly drives his crew to hunt the world's oceans for the great white whale that crippled him. After a long search, the ship encounters the whale and a fierce battle ensues. Finally the captain drives his harpoon into the whale, but the harpoon line catches the captain about the neck and drags him to his death.

A simple story, a straightforward plot—yet, since the 1851 publication of Herman Melville's *Moby-Dick*, readers and critics have found many meanings in the struggle between Captain Ahab and the whale. To some, the novel is a cautionary tale that depicts how Ahab's obsession with revenge leads to his insanity and death. Others believe that the whale represents the unknowable secrets of the universe and that Ahab is a tragic hero who dares to challenge fate by attempting to discover this knowledge. Perhaps Melville intended Ahab as a criticism of Americans' tendency to become involved in well-intentioned but irrational causes. Or did Melville model Ahab after himself, letting his fictional character express his anger at what he perceived as a cruel and distant god?

Although literary critics disagree over the meaning of *Moby-Dick*, readers do not need to choose one particular interpretation in order to gain an understanding of Melville's novel. Instead, by examining various analyses, they can gain numerous insights into the issues that lie under the surface of the basic plot. Studying the writings of literary critics can also aid readers in making their own assessments of *Moby-Dick* and other literary works and in developing analytical thinking skills.

The Greenhaven Literary Companion Series was created with these goals in mind. Designed for young adults, this unique anthology series provides an engaging and comprehensive introduction to literary analysis and criticism. The essays included in the Literary Companion Series are chosen for their accessibility to a young adult audience and are expertly edited in consideration of both the reading and comprehension levels of this audience. In addition, each essay is introduced by a concise summation that presents the contributing writer's main themes and insights. Every anthology in the Literary Companion Series contains a varied selection of critical essays that cover a wide time span and express diverse views. Wherever possible, primary sources are represented through excerpts from authors' notebooks, letters, and journals and through contemporary criticism.

Each title in the Literary Companion Series pays careful consideration to the historical context of the particular author or literary work. In-depth biographies and detailed chronologies reveal important aspects of authors' lives and emphasize the historical events and social milieu that influenced their writings. To facilitate further research, every anthology includes primary and secondary source bibliographies of articles and/or books selected for their suitability for young adults. These engaging features make the Greenhaven Literary Companion Series ideal for introducing students to literary analysis in the classroom or as a library resource for young adults researching the world's great authors and literature.

Exceptional in its focus on young adults, the Greenhaven Literary Companion Series strives to present literary criticism in a compelling and accessible format. Every title in the series is intended to spark readers' interest in leading American and world authors, to help them broaden their understanding of literature, and to encourage them to formulate their own analyses of the literary works that they read. It is the editors' hope that young adult readers will find these anthologies to be true companions in their study of literature.

INTRODUCTION

The evolution of critical opinion of *The Prince and the Pauper* since it was first published in 1881 is a history lesson in itself. The work has been subject to the highest accolades of all of Twain's fiction while also being labeled "a lavish waste of time and talent."[1] Mark Twain's family, his social set, and the literary establishment of the day applauded *The Prince and the Pauper*, his first "serious" novel, as more worthy of his noble character and "kind and sympathetic nature"[2] than the humor and buffoonery of much of his early writing. It was considered a superior example of the historical romance, a fashionable literary mode in England and Europe in the latter part of the nineteenth century. *The Prince and the Pauper* was perceived as a victory in terms of mastery of form for Twain, with a unified structure notably absent from his other books.

Mark Twain took great pride in sending advance copies of the novel elegantly "gotten up" to prominent members of the English and American literary establishment. With the publication of *The Prince and the Pauper*, Twain felt he qualified to be ranked amongst authors of the stature of Charles Dickens and William Makepeace Thackeray. Only Joe Goodman, editor of Nevada's *Enterprise* newspaper, anticipated modern critical reaction when he asked Twain point blank what he was doing "groping among the driftwood of the Deluge for a topic when you would have been so much more at home in the wash of today?"[3]

By the twentieth century, critics who hailed *The Adventures of Tom Sawyer* and *The Adventures of Huckleberry Finn* as masterpieces of American literature damned *The Prince and the Pauper* as a shallow counterfeit work derived from history books. Strong pride in a distinctive American humor, charm, candor, and language led critics like James Cox to claim Twain pandered to the tastes of genteel New England society and betrayed his genius in writing such a book. Published between the more naive *Tom Sawyer* and the more pessimistic *Huckleberry Finn*, these critics saw the principle significance of the work in terms of how it could throw light on Twain's homegrown novels and his development as a social and political reformer, a philosopher, and a literary artist.

Critical controversies centered around whether the book was a "manual of republicanism" focusing on Tom Canty's rise to power or the major expression of Twain's political and cultural conservatism with Edward's restoration as king at the conclusion. In examining its philosophical content, some critics claim the work's underlying pessimism reflecting Twain's interest in human frailty makes it a book principally for adults; others see it as an optimistic, somewhat naive children's book; and still further critics say it reflects Twain's ambiguity on political preferences and wavering on the inherent nature of humanity. Critic Albert Stone says the book was written in response to a call by the literary establishment in the nineteenth century for higher caliber children's fiction that would hold equally absorbing, though differing, messages for children and their parents. Twain's dedication of the work to "Young People of All Ages" has been interpreted as evidence of all of these viewpoints. The book was relegated to the children's section of the library and quietly faded next to the heated controversies over the suitability of *The Adventures of Huckleberry Finn* for the modern American classroom in the latter part of the twentieth century.

"Mark Twain may well be the most representative American writer," said critic Lawrence Howe in 1997, "while what he represents remains eternally open to interpretation."[4] Since the 1990s *The Prince and the Pauper* has been the subject of renewed critical interest. Recent analysis has claimed the work to be on a par with *The Adventures of Huckleberry Finn* and more deeply revealing of the internal conflicts of Samuel Clemens the man than any of his other works. From a psycho-historical perspective, critics see the novel as profoundly significant in understanding Twain, the prevailing American cultural climate, and the very essence of what it means to be an American, then and now. Some view the development and maturing of a postrevolutionary American national identity struggling to break free from European paternalism as a major theme in the novel, which also invokes questions of continuity, succession, legitimacy, and authenticity. With the aim of awakening an abhorrence of injustice, cruelty, abuse of authority, and stifling convention, or, in critic Joe Fulton's words, "fostering an ethical renewal within its readers,"[5] the novel is seen as mainstream Mark Twain. Far from being on the periphery of his contribution to American literature, contemporary critics believe the novel reflects the very heart of Twain's concerns.

Academic controversies aside, the longevity, familiarity, and near-universal appeal of *The Prince and the Pauper* stands as testimony to its worth. It is a book that has enjoyed great popularity on the stage and screen, and it has a plot that children and adults throughout the Western world readily recall, most often with affection. The work has moral force. Themes of mercy, compassion, the fight against injustice, the defeat of evil, and the transformation and triumph of the boy heroes who come through hard life experience is encased in the charm of a fairy tale. Twain's idealism of childhood, the basis of much of the allure of his best books, is at its height in *The Prince and the Pauper.*

NOTES

1. James Cox, *Mark Twain: The Fate of Humor.* Princeton, NJ: Princeton University Press, 1966, p. 149.
2. Quoted in Susy Clemens, *Papa: An Intimate Biography of Mark Twain.* Ed. Charles Neider. New York: Doubleday, 1985, p. 33.
3. Quoted in Kenneth Andrews, *Nook Farm: Mark Twain's Hartford Circle.* Cambridge, MA: Harvard University Press, 1950, p. 192.
4. Lawrence Howe, *Mark Twain and the Novel: The Double Cross of Authority.* New York: Cambridge University Press, 1998, p. 14.
5. Joe Fulton, *Mark Twain's Ethical Realism.* Columbia: University of Missouri Press, 1997, p. 146.

Mark Twain: A Biography

When Halley's comet reached its closest proximity to the sun before being hurled back out into the solar system in 1835, a fifth child, two months premature, was born to John M. and Jane L. Clemens in a two-room frame house with a lean-to kitchen in the modest town of Florida, Missouri. It was a humble beginning for Samuel Langhorne Clemens, the man who would invent the persona of Mark Twain. Yet Twain was to become, in the words of literary critic H.L. Mencken, "by long odds, the largest figure that ever reared itself out of the flat, damp prairie of American literature."[1]

THE AMERICAN CONTEXT

During Samuel Clemens's lifetime (1835–1910), America underwent tremendous growth, change, and turmoil. Peoples' lives were radically altered. The United States shifted from an agrarian- to an industrial-based economy. Large-scale industrialization and capitalism led to massive migration to burgeoning urban centers. Westward migration, hastened by the discovery of gold and precious metals, opened up the western frontier. The United States survived foreign wars and a civil war, and the institution of slavery was abolished, giving citizenship to those formerly in bondage but not ensuring them equality. Democracy was the object of great national pride and deep disillusionment, given the reality of discrimination and political corruption. But America was moving forward. The railroad boosted the economy. The telephone and telegraph revolutionized communication. By the end of the century, the United States, once a colony itself, was a world power making imperialist moves to claim territories outside its borders.

Samuel Clemens witnessed the extraordinary transformation of both his country and his countrymen. He was intimately connected with world affairs, national politics, and, through his colorful life experiences and giant propensity for compassion, the common American. His generation bridged the gap between a stable and unstable America. The central dilemma of nineteenth-century thought was reflected in the conflicting beliefs of faith in the perfectibility of humanity through the new democratic institutions and scientific progress versus the dogma that human nature is static, rigid, and molded by uncontrollable forces. Clemens's works reflect this dilemma and echo the pain of changing times. They reveal much about an evolving national culture and character, proud, defiant, and fraught with insecurities and contradiction.

FAMILY AND HERITAGE

"I was born," Clemens later wrote, "on the 30th of November, 1835, in the almost invisible village of Florida, Monroe County, Missouri. My parents removed to Missouri in the early 'thirties; I do not remember just when, for I was not born then and cared nothing for such things. It was a long journey and must have been a rough and tiresome one. The village contained a hundred people and I increased the population by one per cent. It is more than many of the best men in history could have done for a town. It may not be modest of me to refer to this but it is true. There is no record of a person doing as much—not even Shakespeare. But I did it for Florida and it shows that I could have done it for any place—even London, I suppose."[2]

Young Sam Clemens grew up in a household proud of its distinguished English ancestral heritage. Jane Clemens claimed to be a descendant of the Lambtons of England, earls of Durham, and John Clemens traced his roots back to Judge Gregory Clement, one of the judges who sentenced King Charles I to death—or, as Sam was later to boast, "did what he could toward reducing the list of crowned shams of his day."[3]

Sam was the fifth child after Orion, the eldest boy; Pamela; Margaret; and Benjamin. His younger brother, Henry, was three years his junior. John and Jane Clemens came from Virginia families and considered themselves gentry, or upper-class landowners. John was a lawyer by training, a farmer and merchant by necessity, and a speculator by temperament. Although he was known as a man of integrity, actively involved in the affairs of the community, he did not excel as a provider or as a father. Sam's childhood was marked by a series of financial reversals. After his father's inaccurate projection that Florida, Missouri, with its pivotal position on the Salt River, would become a boomtown, the family moved in 1837 to the nearby town of Hannibal, close to Jane's sister and brother-in-law, Patsy and Charles Quarles. Sam's experiences on the Quarles's farm was the basis for some of his finest fiction. John Clemens's repeated failure at commercial ventures, coupled with a loan to an unreliable recipient, gave Sam the experience of financial hardship in his youth. At times things were so tight that they had to sell the family furniture, and in 1846 they were compelled to share living quarters with another family, for whom Jane did the cooking.

Austere was the principal adjective Samuel Clemens used to describe his father. He recalled him as being "stern, unsmiling, never demonstrating affection for wife or child . . . ungentle of manner towards his children . . . [though he] never punished—a look was enough, and more than enough."[4] Biographer John Lauber describes an incident that occurred when the rest of the family had gone to the Quarles's farm and left seven-year-old Sam in his father's charge. Early the next morning John Clemens rode off, forgetting his young son. Several hours later a rescuer arrived to find Sam locked in the house and "crying with loneliness and hunger."[5] According to critic John Stahl, the author's focus on father-son relationships in his fiction drew breath from the early childhood experiences of a sensitive young boy with a stern and dismissive father.

Sam's recollections of his mother were warmer and more emotional. She was a person with "a heart so large that everybody's griefs and everybody's joys found welcome in its hospitable accommodation."[6] Jane Clemens had a strong and inquisitive interest in everybody and everything. Her courage and compassion were evident in one incident when a mean-spirited father, well-known as the town bully, chased his daughter through the streets of Hannibal with a whip in his hands claiming he would beat her mercilessly. No one dared interfere until Jane Clemens opened her house to the fleeing girl, then stood in the doorway and faced down the brutal father, who, Sam recalled, said "with a great and blasphemous oath that she was the bravest woman he ever saw and went away."[7]

Biographers claim Sam drew his zest for life, strong sense of humor, and compassion for the oppressed from his mother.

With John Clemens, Sam shared a strong intellect and personal integrity, a love of language, an active involvement in affairs of the world, and dreams of great wealth that came to naught.

EARLY REBELLIOUSNESS

Sam's physical frailty as a young child seemed to have had little effect on his precocious spirit. He would later say that he furnished his mother with some variety from the "unbroken monotony of [his younger brother] Henry's goodness and truthfulness."[8] One often-recited incident happened during an outbreak of an epidemic of measles in Hannibal when he was nine. Unable to stand the suspense as to whether he would come down with the deadly disease, Sam finally managed to become infected after his second attempt at jumping into a friend's sickbed. He came close to joining the ranks of the one in two children who did not survive to reach adulthood, but he was mercifully spared. His siblings were less fortunate. Margaret and Benjamin were fatally stricken with common childhood illnesses at the ages of nine and ten, respectively.

To Sam's restless and imaginative spirit, school was a stifling bore. On his first day he broke a rule and was moved to another school. He later described school as a place where children "devoted . . . eight or ten hours a day to learning incomprehensible rubbish by heart out of books and reciting it by rote, like parrots."[9] Sam excelled in spelling bees but little else. According to biographer John Lauber, school "sought to inculcate the virtues of industry, patriotism and piety" in Sam. "It tried to make him a Model boy and failed utterly. His real education would come later."[10]

On Sundays, Sam further exasperated his mother by finding diversions by the river on his way to church. Despite his truancy, he did receive a thorough religious indoctrination supervised by his mother. A deep fear and terror of damnation and hell was instilled early in young Sam and is seen as the source of his guilty conscience and overdeveloped sense of responsibility, which plagued him during his lifetime. He later described the sermons of the Presbyterian minister as both sleep-inducing and full of arguments that "dealt in limitless fire and brimstone and thinned the predestined elect down to a company so small as to be hardly worth saving." He also railed strongly against the Presbyterianism of the

Mississippi Valley as an institution that "demanded perfectionism while insisting on the total depravity of the human race, giving to God the power and the right, in His inscrutable wisdom, to save those whom He chose to save and damn those whom He chose to damn."[11]

MISSOURI BOYHOOD

Life on the Mississippi River, which is graphically depicted in his best-known works, shaped Sam's childhood. Tremendous romance surrounded the two-chimneyed paddle-wheel boats with elevated pilot houses that clattered and clamored down the river. The monotony of small-town life was relieved by the flurry of excitement as people and merchandise were hurriedly loaded and unloaded onto the docks. A "permanent ambition" of the boys living on the river was to become a steamboat pilot—an ambition that later would become a reality for Sam and many of his childhood friends.

His boyhood summers at the Quarles's farm also colored his life and his writings. He would recall in "Early Days" (1897–98),

> I spent some part of the year at the farm until I was twelve or thirteen years old. The life which I led there with my cousins was full of charm, and so is the memory of it yet. I can call back the solemn twilight and mystery of the deep woods, the earthy smells, the faint odors of the wild flowers, the sheen of rain-washed foliage, the rattling clatter of drops when the wind shook the trees, the far-off hammering of woodpeckers and the muffled drumming of wood pheasants in the remoteness of the forest, the snapshot glimpses of disturbed wild creatures scurrying through the grass—I can call it back and make it as real as it ever was, and as blessed.[12]

Sam had strong, fond memories of the slaves on his uncle's farm. A middle-aged slave known as "Uncle Dan'l" was a pivotal figure of his youth. Clemens later said of him,

> He was a man whose sympathies were wide and warm and whose heart was honest and simple and knew no guile. He has served me well these many, many years. I have not seen him for more than half a century and yet spiritually I have had his welcome company a good part of that time and have staged him in books under his own name and as "Jim" and carted him all around—to Hannibal, down the Mississippi on a raft and even across the desert of the Sahara in a balloon—and he has endured it all with patience and friendliness and loyalty which is his birthright. It was on the farm that I got my strong liking for his race and my appreciation of certain of his

fine qualities. This feeling and this estimate have stood the test of sixty years and more and suffered no impairment. The black face is as welcome to me now as it was then.[13]

Slavery was a fact of Missouri life, and as a child Sam Clemens had no aversion to it. He later wrote, "I was not aware that there was anything wrong with it. . . . [Even] the local pulpit taught us that God approved it and it was a holy thing."[14] However, disturbing scenes of slave families being forcibly separated left strong impressions on him. He once complained to his mother of the constant "singing, whistling, whooping, laughing" of a young slave boy called Sandy who was in their employ. "When he sings," she replied gently, "he shows that he is not remembering and that comforts me; but when he is still I am afraid he is thinking and I cannot bear it. He will never see his mother again; if he can sing I must not hinder it, but be thankful for it." According to Clemens, "It was a simple speech and made up of small words but it went home, and Sandy's noise was not a trouble to me anymore."[15]

In later life Clemens came to abhor racial prejudice. He sponsored scholarships for black students, and in "Which Is It?" he tells the story from the viewpoint of blacks in the Deep South demonstrating with vehemence his mature and firm belief in the basic human right to equal and just treatment.

INTELLECTUAL AWAKENING

In 1847 Clemens's childhood days came to an abrupt halt with the sudden death his father. On the verge of commencing his appointment to the lucrative position of clerk to the Surrogate Court, John Clemens contracted pleurisy from inclement weather and died, leaving the family destitute. Despite their distant relationship, Sam was overcome with guilt about the times he had defied his father's wishes. He made an oath to his mother, pledging to be a faithful, industrious, and upright man like his father. Clemens's official biographer, A.B. Paine, maintains that this oath shaped much of Clemens's adult life: "The sense of honor was strong within him. To him a promise was a serious matter; made under conditions like these it would be held sacred."[16]

Following the death of his father, Clemens's brother Orion returned to St. Louis to resume his work as a printer. After a couple of years of attending school probably part-time, Sam was persuaded by his mother to follow Orion's lead and become a printer's apprentice. He was in good company. Noted writers like Walt Whitman, William Dean Howells, and Bret Harte all began their literary careers in printing offices, generally recognized as the poor man's university in nineteenth-century America. The literary articles and poetry that were printed in newspapers of the times became a source of a more effective education than the formal schoolhouse had ever been for Samuel Clemens. Paine suggests that Clemens's lifelong fascination with history was sparked at this time, by a chance incident when he found a scrap of paper out of a book about Joan of Arc flying along the pavement. With little previous exposure to history, Clemens was captivated by the plight of the gentle maid of Orleans. "From that moment when that fluttering leaf was blown into his hands," writes Paine, "his career as one of the world's mentally elect was assured. It gave him his cue—the first word in the part of a human drama. It crystallized suddenly within him sympathy with the oppressed, rebellion against tyranny and treachery, scorn for the divine right of kings."[17] *The Prince and the Pauper*, *Personal Recollections of Joan of Arc*, and *A Connecticut Yankee in King Arthur's Court* were direct products of that interest in history that began when Clemens was in his late teens. Although as a literary personality Clemens liked to masquerade as uneducated and even ignorant, he read history, philosophy, science, classical literature, and works by the major thinkers of his time. His spirit of enquiry was wide and far-reaching, and he was an impressive example of the self-educated man.

A Writer's Beginnings

After a brief apprenticeship with Joseph Ament of the *Hannibal Courier*, Clemens took up his brother Orion's offer to work at the newly purchased *Hannibal Western Union*. Though the paper never flourished or paid him any of the promised wages, Clemens did get the opportunity to appear in print for the first time. He modeled his first writing efforts on a distinctly American form of humor that was growing in popularity. This featured rogues, confidence men, and exaggerated tall tales with a main theme relating to the distinction between the real and the false or the pretentious and the unsophisticated. "Clemens found this concern with victimization and humiliation particularly congenial to his talents and attitudes,"[18] writes biographer Everett Emerson.

"A Gallant Fireman," Clemens's first published work, appeared in the *Western Union* on January 16, 1851. It was one paragraph describing the "heroics" of a young printer's apprentice who thought himself worthy of being immortalized after removing a few odd and worthless items from the print shop in response to a fire in the grocery store next door. In May of the following year, "The Dandy Frightening the Squatter" was published in the *Boston Carpet-Bag*, which contained the familiar theme of a proper and pretentious easterner making a fool of himself by challenging a man from the frontier. The article included expressions of strong local dialects that foreshadowed the language in Clemens's later works. A week later the *Philadelphia* printed Clemens's description of Hannibal. "A joy which rather exceeded anything in that line I have ever experienced since,"[19] was how Clemens described seeing his first efforts given recognition.

A Contentious, Irreverent Style

In an effort to add a bit of spice and boost the flagging sales of the *Hannibal Western Union*, much to his brother's consternation, Clemens took advantage of Orion's absence from home in September 1852 to write several contentious articles that outraged local residents. These included one piece mocking the efforts of a rival editor who had resolved to commit suicide by drowning in Bear Creek after being jilted. His suicide note was found by a would-be rescuer, who arrived in time to see him walk out of the muddy waters having lost his nerve. These derisive articles angered many people, including the *Western Union*'s editor, but the provocation paid off. Thirty-three new subscribers were added to the paper's circulation.

By 1855, like many humorists of the day, Clemens began to write under a range of pen names, including W. Epaminondas Adrastus Perkins, the Rambler, the Grumbler, and John Snooks. He wrote jokes, puns, hoaxes, and started feuds with rival editors in town. Although Clemens was eventually given his own column, the lack of pay and continued strains with his brother encouraged him to venture farther afield. At the age of eighteen Clemens left Hannibal, Missouri, and took off into the wide world.

New York, Philadelphia, and St. Louis

After a short stint in St. Louis with his sister, Clemens went to New York and worked as a typesetter in a printing office. Continuing his self-education, he took advantage of the libraries accessible to printers and read voraciously in the evenings. Clemens soon moved on to Philadelphia, and from there he wrote a series of letters for Iowa's *Muscatine Journal*, including his first travel writing. Under financial strain, he returned to St. Louis, where his mother now lived with his sister. While visiting Orion, who had married and moved to Keokuk, Iowa, Clemens spoke at a printers' banquet. He first demonstrated his aptitude for public speaking at the 150th anniversary of the birth of Benjamin Franklin, the patron saint of American printers.

In the summer of 1856 Clemens began writing a series of letters under the pen name Thomas Jefferson Snodgrass. Snodgrass was from the backwaters, an innocent and ready victim of his city adventures. The first letter tells of the country bumpkin's impressions of Shakespeare's *Julius Caesar*. The last of the Snodgrass letters was written when Clemens was twenty-one. According to Emerson, the Snodgrass letters were not significant in the development of Clemens's unique style, though they did demonstrate his desire to be a humorous writer. "I have a call to literature of a low order i.e. humorous," he was later to write to Orion, "it is nothing to be proud of but it is my strongest suit."[20]

THE ROOTS OF HIS PHILOSOPHICAL THOUGHT

Clemens spent the winter of 1856–1857 in Cincinnati working at the printing office of Wrightson and Company. He lived in a cheap boardinghouse, where he met a Scotsman named Macfarlane. A man of sober character, serious demeanor, and sharp intellect, Macfarlane had an impressive personal library of historical, philosophical, and scientific works, many of which he knew by heart. Macfarlane had developed his own views independent of Charles Darwin, and he believed that man had grown from a microscopic seedgerm planted by God at the dawn of time. He believed that something had gone wrong when man was the only species capable of malice, vindictiveness, drunkenness, and placing other men in servitude and captivity. Long discussions with Macfarlane late into the night left a strong impression on Clemens, who was to reiterate many of these same notions and bitter pessimism in *What Is Man?* published anonymously in the early twentieth century. The depravity of the human race was a theme that came through Clemens's fictional works late in his life.

THE CALL OF THE RIVER

Restlessness in his veins, Clemens bought a ticket to New Orleans in April 1857 aboard the steamboat *Paul Jones*. Before the journey was concluded he had charmed and cajoled the stern and grumbly pilot, Horace Bixby, into teaching him how to navigate the Mississippi. For the next four years, Clemens fulfilled his childhood ambition and piloted the massive steamboats up and down the river. Many of his old pals from Hannibal were also pilots. Clemens recalled an early episode in his training under Bixby: "One day he turned to me suddenly with this settler: 'What is the shape of Walnut Bend?' He might as well have asked me my Grandmother's opinion of protoplasm." Bixby went on to describe at length how the young pilot must learn every twist and turn in the river by heart so that he could navigate it on a pitch-black night. He further explained that the river assumed different shapes throughout the day and that it appeared differently in moonlight than it did on a dark night. What's more, the shape was constantly changing and these changes must also be memorized. Finally Clemens exclaimed, "When I can do all that, I'll be able to raise the dead, and then I won't have to pilot a steamboat to make a living."[21] Clemens's descriptions of his experiences with Bixby, with some exaggeration, were the basis for his most brilliant passages in *Old Times on the Mississippi* (1875).

Critics have sought to explain what motivated the dreamy and undetail-oriented Clemens to master the complex navigation of the Mississippi. Biographer Paine maintains that Clemens's deep love of the river and his desire for the considerable prestige of being a pilot drove the unlikely candidate. A pilot could be a gentleman while a typesetter could not. The steamboat business was in its heyday, providing the main lines for carrying cargo and passengers from the Gulf of New Orleans. Steamboat pilots earned wages equal to the vice president of the United States. The prestige, authority, and independence attracted Clemens. He later said that all men but the steamboat pilot "are slaves to other men and circumstances."[22]

Linked with these memories of Clemens's glory days was the tragedy of his brother Henry's death following a boiler explosion on the *Pennsylvania*. After an altercation with a crew member, Sam Clemens had left the boat and was thus spared the deadly accident. He was forever plagued by a sense of guilt for his survival and for his role in encouraging Henry to work on steamboats. Emerson suggests that Clemens's overdeveloped guilty conscience, the basis for much of his personal suffering, was linked to his attraction to the philosophy of determinism. If forces in the external environment largely determined man's fate, then one's level of personal responsibility could be denied or diminished.

THE CIVIL WAR YEARS

In January 1861 Clemens's four-year career as a steamboat pilot came to an abrupt halt when two warning shots were blasted through the chimneys of the *Nebraska*, smattering glass from the pilothouse in which he stood. The *Nebraska* was the last boat to pass through the union blockade of the Mississippi River. The reality of war hit home.

In the presidential election of 1860, Clemens voted for John Bell of Tennessee, a member of the Constitutional Union Party, which stood for both the Union and slavery. Bell was the candidate of choice for many of the residents of border states like Missouri, which subsequently became the battleground of fierce conflicts between troops from the North and the South.

Clemens returned to Hannibal and joined a small band of his boyhood friends who called themselves the Marion Rangers (Hannibal is in Marion County). They adopted the Confederate cause and dreamed of heroic fights and hard-won glory. Clemens later described the distinguishing characteristics of his band members in *The Private History of a Campaign That Failed* as "young, ignorant, good-natured, well-meaning, trivial, full of romance, and given to reading chivalric novels and singing forlorn love-ditties." He went on to say,

> [This] is a not unfair picture of what went on in many and many a militia camp in the first months of the rebellion, when the green recruits were without discipline, without the steadying and heartening influence of trained leaders, when all their circumstances were new and strange and charged with exaggerated terrors, and before the invaluable experience of actual collision in the field had turned them from rabbits into soldiers. I could have become a soldier myself if I had waited. I had got part of it learned, I knew more about retreating than the man that invented retreating.[23]

General Fremont, commander of the Union forces in Missouri, ordered the freeing of slaves in August 1861, but President Abraham Lincoln reversed him in an effort to hold the loyalty of the border state, which had not seceded from the Union. Bloody conflicts were fought between neighbors in once peaceful Hannibal, but by this time Clemens had "resigned" from the Confederate army after two-weeks' service, claiming he was "incapacitated by fatigue through persistent retreating."[24] His service was considered too informal and irregular for it to be said that he was a deserter, but it did come back to haunt him. His "brief and inglorious" military career with the Confederates was looked upon askance by some of his future companions from the Eastern upper class, who were diehard abolitionists. But he was in good company. Most of the major American writers of the post-Civil War period, like William Dean Howells, Henry James, and Henry Adams, elected to stay clear of footsoldiering.

CLEMENS THE RENEGADE WESTERNER

In July 1861 Clemens accompanied Orion to Carson City, Nevada. Orion had been appointed secretary of the Nevada Territory by a personal friend, Edward Bates, Lincoln's secretary-general. The state of Nevada was created in February of the same year from land taken during the Mexican-American War. The discovery of silver had heightened the sense of urgency to dispatch officials to the new territory. After a long, dusty, and memorable stagecoach journey, later to provide colorful material for *Roughing It*, they arrived in Carson City.

Finding no employment related to his brother's position, Clemens devoted himself to the observation and study of human nature on the frontier. Paine colorfully describes him in this new context:

> He quickly adapted himself to frontier mode. Lately a river sovereign and dandy, in fancy percales and patent leathers, he had become the roughest of rough-clad pioneers, in rusty slouch hat, flannel shirt, coarse trousers slopping half in and half out of the heavy cow-skin boots. Always something of a barbarian in love with the loose habit of unconvention, he went even further than others and became a sort of paragon of disarray.[25]

By the early winter, Clemens yielded to the epidemic of mining fever and was, in his own words, "as frenzied as the craziest."[26] Although this escapade provided further fuel for his future literary works, it totally failed to provide the promised riches. Clemens's mining ambitions died hard while his get-rich-quick fever went into remission to emerge later in his life with similar result.

Long letters home describing his frontier adventures were the basis of his first pieces sent to a variety of newspapers, including Nevada's leading paper, the *Territorial Enterprise*. In 1862 the paper's editor and Clemens's soon-to-be loyal friend, Joseph Goodman, offered him a job as a staff journalist. In the face of dire financial circumstances and his serious disappointment about his failed mining enterprise, Clemens agreed to take up the job in Virginia City.

THE BIRTH OF MARK TWAIN

"Washoe [as Nevada was then called] perfectly satisfied and agreed with the compositor-pilot-prospector who here came into his heritage," says critic Bernard DeVoto.

> It was Washoe that matured Sam Clemens, that gave him, after three false apprenticeships, the trade he would follow all his life, and that brought into harmony the elements of his mind which before had fumbled for expression. In the desert air a writer grew to maturity.[27]

Clemens became a successful journalist in the boom-or-bust atmosphere of Virginia City. He covered the Nevada state legislature, the main distinguishing features of which were, according to Paine, "ignorance of procedures, a wide latitude of speech, a noble appreciation of humor, and plenty of brains."[28] It was a fitting training ground, and Clemens made no bones about spicing up his reports on the legislative activities.

During these Nevada years, Clemens created his first fully developed character to flout gentility. When a rival reporter wrote a disparaging article about one of Clemens's reports on the legislature, Clemens replied that it was "a festering mass of misstatements the author of whom should be properly termed, 'the Unreliable.'"[29] Thereafter, "the Unreliable" became a pseudonym Clemens used to express that part of him that railed against convention and was repulsed by sentimentality. In one article, he visits San Francisco with the Unreliable, who borrows Clemens's most elegant clothes and, masquerading in his guise, goes to a party, gets hopelessly drunk, eats a whole roast pig, sings a drunken song, and swindles the hotel where they are both lodged. According to Emerson, through the use of such literary characters as the Unreliable, "the developing author was seeking a means of expressing himself frankly but without sullying himself."[30]

The first recorded use of Clemens's famous pseudonym, Mark Twain, was in a newsletter published on February 3, 1863. Like the humorists of his day, Clemens felt he needed an individuality in order to build a reputation. Technically, *mark twain* is a riverboat term of measurement indicating there is twelve feet of water below the vessel's waterline. This depth was the dividing line between safe and dangerously shallow water for steamboats. Clemens claimed to have taken the name from a pilot, Isaiah Sellers, who wrote unexceptional articles under the name Mark Twain. Clemens had satirized and so embarrassed some of Sellers's work years before in his river days that Sellers had ended his literary efforts. Partly out of remorse and homage to Sellers, Clemens adopted the name after Sellers's death. Schol-

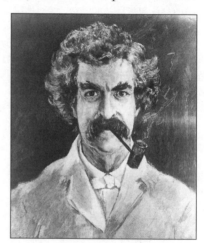

ars have offered alternate explanations for the choice of the pseudonym. Some have suggested a link with the Old English meaning of *twain*, representing two, and the author's interest in duality. Others have specu-lated that in signifying the presence of safe water, it was a comfort to the au-thor. Truth or fiction, it was the name Clemens was to adopt in early 1863. He would eventually develop an entire persona around

Mark Twain

this term he carried from his days on the Mississippi.

While working for Nevada's *Enterprise*, Mark Twain real-ized the close connection between the comic and the forbid-den and understood that humor relaxed a repressive atmos-phere. He had more difficulty, however, in working out how far he could go without offense. According to Emerson, "He sensed he could amusingly violate inhibiting strictures by sat-irizing the fastidiousness of the genteel and their attitudes to-wards romantic love, childhood, grand opera, admiration for the 'sublime' in nature, even benevolent humanitarianism."[51]

In the spring of 1864, Twain went too far. After writing a piece that offended a Civil War organization (akin to the Red Cross) by suggesting that funds were being embezzled, he became a persona non grata and had to leave the territory. In that brief period of eighteen months in Nevada after taking the name of Mark Twain, Clemens had become a well-known, though perhaps notorious, western humorist.

CALIFORNIA

When Twain moved to Virginia City, he was considered an amusing but indolent man of no renown. By the time of his hurried departure, he was seen as a person of consequence. The flowering of Mark Twain as an authorial identity was sharply curbed by his move to San Francisco in 1864. As a reporter for the *Morning Call*, he had a grueling schedule from dawn until midnight covering the events of the city, from the police courts to drama-critic reporting on several theatrical shows a night, often straining to bring back adequate copy to fill the next day's news. The editor found Twain's slow drawl and slovenly style not to his liking, and when a young, bright-eyed, and bushy-tailed journalist was brought on the staff, he suggested Twain consider resigning. Twain gladly obliged. He had begun writing for the San Francisco *Californian*, a more sophisticated literary paper, through which he met the editor, Bret Harte. A well-established writer of the time, Harte thought Twain's best pieces were equivalent to those of Charles Dickens, and Twain became the most highly paid contributor to the *Californian*. At the encouragement of renowned humorist Artemus Ward, he began to send articles to eastern newspapers. The *New York Weekly Review* published eight pieces in 1865 and 1866, the first being an account of the San Francisco earthquake of October 7. Mark Twain had begun to build his reputation in the East.

Twain continued as Californian correspondent for the Nevada *Enterprise* and published several pieces criticizing the San Francisco police for corruption and ineptitude. He abhorred the abuse and intimidation of Chinese immigrants and wrote strong pieces in their defense. He finally became so unpopular with the San Francisco police that he left for Calaveras County, where he dug for gold, without result. However, the experience proved a valuable one as the local miners' tales he heard became the basis for his first longer piece, which was published as "The Jumping Frog of Calaveras County" in 1867.

Restless and strapped for funds, Twain decided to take a trip as a paid correspondent to the Sandwich Islands, as Hawaii was then known. And so began his early travel writings that would later flower into works like *The Innocents Abroad.* The trip to Hawaii was significant on another count. In California and Nevada, Twain was known as something of a renegade, writing satires about the dominant culture—the politicians, the clergy, and police force. Emerson notes, "He was an outsider, a bohemian. As a writer he was a hoaxer and a humorist, a man of limited education and uncertain ambition. All this was to change [after his trip to Hawaii], at least on the surface."[32] In Hawaii he met people of importance, such as Anson Burlingame, U.S. envoy to China. "Avoid inferiors" was Burlingame's advice. "Seek your comradeships among superiors in intellect and character. Always climb."[33] Twain took this advice seriously. "Samuel Clemens would climb," notes Emerson, "sometimes leaving Mark Twain far behind, often with unfortunate results for the writer—and perhaps also for the person."[34]

THE RETURN EAST

Upon his return to San Francisco, Twain capitalized on his Hawaiian experiences and had his first paid public lecture for about eighteen hundred people. His success as a public speaker, his reputation as a humorist, and his tremendous personal popularity took him on a lecture circuit of Nevada and California and in years to come became his means of digging himself out of financial straits.

Twain departed for New York in January 1867. There, he met up with Charles Webb, an old acquaintance who agreed to publish his first book, *The Celebrated Jumping Frog of Calaveras County and Other Sketches.* Critics have noted that the book was not a strong example of Twain's literary identity, which was to be revealed more forcefully in later novels. He was disappointed in the financial return on the work, and continuing to judge himself harshly, he wrote to his mother that he was "so worthless that it seems to me I never do anything or accomplish anything that lingers in my mind as a pleasant memory."[35]

TURNING POINT

In June 1867 Twain had the good fortune to be paid by the *Alta California* to travel aboard the *Quaker City,* the first transatlantic steamship to carry American tourists to the Mediterranean and the Holy Land. The series of letters he wrote during the trip became the basis for his novel *The In-nocents Abroad.* His letters were humorous, irreverent, and tended to note the superiority of America to Old World values and traditions. However, as the voyage progressed, his correspondence began to be more refined and less outrageous, largely owing to the active editing by a fellow journalist and socialite from Cleveland, Ohio, Mary Mason Fairbanks. Twain later explained, "Coming home I cramped myself down to at least something like decency of expression, and wrote some twenty letters, which have survived the examination of a most fastidious censor on shipboard and are consequently not incendiary documents."[36] Fairbanks's editing of Twain's natural outrageousness was the first of a number of influences that refined Twain's style and the rougher edges of his work.

ROMANCE

During the voyage of the *Quaker City,* Twain first saw a miniature portrait of Olivia Langdon, the sister of a shipboard acquaintance, Charles Langdon. Twain was instantly captured by the miniature of the frail and pretty Langdon. He worshiped her from their first meeting in December 1867. Langdon's reaction to Twain, however, was less sanguine. According to Paine,

> He disturbed rather than gratified her. She sensed his heresy towards the conventions and forms which had been her gospel; his bantering indifferent attitude towards life—to her always so serious and sacred; she suspected that he might even have unorthodox views on matters of religion. When he had gone she somehow had the feeling that a great fiery meteor of unknown portent had swept across her sky.[37]

The Langdon clan took a good deal of convincing that Twain was a suitable match for Olivia. They were the epitome of the genteel eastern set that Twain's work had long satirized. Her father, Jervis Langdon, asked for character witnesses, who almost wrecked the marital plans. One Presbyterian minister claimed, "I would rather bury a daughter of mine than have her marry such a fellow"[38] and another witness predicted Twain would fill "a pauper's grave."[39] But against such evidence, Jervis Langdon said, "I'll be your friend myself. Take the girl. I know you better than they do."[40] To meet the approval of her family, Twain became a practicing Christian and initially went to church and read the Bible with Olivia (or "Livy" as he came to call her). After reflecting on his experiences in the Holy Land, however, Twain found Christianity hypocritical and abandoned it. Eventually Olivia did likewise.

Olivia's role as editor in Twain's writing began with *The Innocents Abroad*, which the publisher, Elisha Bliss Jr., suggested he write upon his return to the United States. The work did demonstrate Twain's ability to observe foreigners and see himself through their eyes, and in so doing, according to critic Joe Fulton, "gain insight about his own character, and about the American character."[41] In late 1869 Twain met William Dean Howells, an editor of the *Atlantic* at the time, who favorably reviewed *The Innocents Abroad*. Howells saw the genius in Twain's work early on and became a valuable ally and editor throughout Twain's career.

THE NOOK FARM YEARS

In 1870 Twain and Langdon married and moved to a new home in the Nook Farm area of Hartford, Connecticut, which had been a surprise wedding gift from Jervis Langdon. The 1870s and 1880s in Nook Farm was a period of stability and domesticity as Twain relished being a devoted father to his three daughters (their firstborn and only son, Langdon, died before the age of two), glowed with the many friendships in his environment, and from all accounts experienced marital bliss with Livy. The ideal of a happy family life permeated the neighborhood, and Twain seemed to thrive amidst the lavish hospitality and many social obligations that consumed his time. His writing was confined for the most part to their summer vacations at Elmira in New York. Many of his peers found the brilliance Twain exhibited in his social encounters greater than that displayed in his books. He was happy, content, and seemingly well adjusted. In 1874 he wrote, "If there is one individual creature on all this footstool who is more thoroughly and uniformly and unceasingly happy than I am, I defy the world to produce him. In my opinion he doesn't exist."[42]

Despite his limited time writing, in the twenty years after his marriage he coauthored with Charles Dudley Warner *The Gilded Age*, which gave the period its name, and produced *The Adventures of Tom Sawyer*, *A Tramp Abroad*, *The Prince and the Pauper*, *The Adventures of Huckleberry Finn*, and *A Connecticut Yankee in King Arthur's Court*, amongst a host of minor works.

NOOK FARM INTELLECTUAL LIFE

There was a strong intellectual life in the Nook Farm area, which included not only the professional writers but also revered members of Hartford society. The Monday Evening Club became a forum for Twain to express his religious and social views uncensored by Livy or his friends. From all accounts, his unconventional opinions met with verbal disagreement but not personal disapproval. However, based on the reaction of this sample group, Twain chose to withhold some of his darker views from the general public as he held an abhorrence for public disapproval and censure.

Nook Farm was the home of two other authors of note besides Mark Twain. Both Harriet Beecher Stowe (*Uncle Tom's Cabin*) and Charles Dudley Warner (a well-known author in those times) shared with Twain their status as professional writers rather than deliberate artists. As such, quantity and public taste were the major considerations in what they chose to write. Twain was known to abandon what is today acknowledged as his finest work—*The Adventures of Huckleberry Finn*—while devoting time to inferior works to capitalize on his income from writing. Despite the large quantity of such poorer works, the Nook Farm authors—Twain, Stowe, and Warner—wrote some fine literature, which derived its power from times past, evoking the simpler, preindustrial society of their childhoods. According to biographer Kenneth Andrews,

> The Classics emerging from the environmental uneasiness beneath the surface placidity of Nook Farm stem more directly from the pain of changing worlds than from all the literary truths lavished on trash and truth alike. Beautiful in the distance beyond the Civil War and peaceful in contrast to the kaleidoscopic present, youth remembered is the emotional source of Nook Farm Literature.[43]

THE UNRAVELING

As the 1880s progressed, the financial pressures of maintaining an enormous household became a burden. Twain wrote of an "intermittent badgered, harassed feeling. . . . It comes mainly of business responsibilities and annoyances."[44] Duplicating his quest for gold out west, but in a more sophisticated setting, Twain embarked on speculations of a great variety that ultimately turned into a frantic scrambling to pay his bills. Struck with the same get-rich-quick fever and faulty judgment as his father, Twain sponsored over a hundred inventions, including the Paige typesetting machine, convinced that great riches were within his reach. As each of these failed, and after he exhausted Livy's family endowment, his pleasure in Hartford society was undermined. By the end of the 1880s, with debts of enormous proportion, the family was forced to close down the house and head for Europe, where Twain planned to earn money on the lecture circuit. The family spent the best part of the 1890s living in Europe.

THE DECLINING YEARS

The sense of equilibrium that Twain had achieved in the early 1880s was gone by the 1890s. As his personal life and fortunes took him into profound unhappiness, it became more difficult for Mark Twain to exude the same special qualities notable in such works as *The Adventures of Huckleberry Finn.* As he closely observed the greed of the Gilded Age, political corruption, imperialist moves by the United States with which he strongly disagreed, and the dislocation of his times, his pessimism grew. He became disheartened with humanity and began to decry historical progress and see human history as comprising the endless return of evil.

"For a time he could take baseness and indecency in stride and accept their role even in the enchantment of the river,"[45] writes Andrews. But with a series of personal tragedies, including his mother's death in 1890, the sudden death of his favorite daughter, Susy, in 1896, the passing of Orion in 1897, and Livy's death in 1904, he could no longer withstand his pessimistic tendencies. Despite ill health, Twain made his final trip to Europe in 1907 for the purpose of accepting an honorary degree from Oxford University, which he considered a crowning achievement. In 1909 his daughter Clara moved to Europe, and Twain settled down with his youngest daughter, Jean. On Christmas Eve of that year, Jean suffered an epileptic seizure and drowned in her bath.

On April 20, 1910, Halley's comet returned to circle the sun. Twain had often said he expected to go out with the comet's return: "I came in with Halley's comet in 1835. It is coming again next year and it will be the greatest disappointment of my life if I don't go out with it. . . . The Almighty said, no doubt: 'Now here are these two unaccountable freaks; they came in together, they must go out together.'"[46]

Having made up his mind to go out with the celestial event, Mark Twain promptly died at midday on April 21, 1910.

THE DUAL PERSONAS OF SAMUEL CLEMENS AND MARK TWAIN

One of the last coherent references Twain made on his deathbed was to the infamous Dr. Jekyll and Mr. Hyde. Mark Twain's fascination with dual personalities, doubles, twins, frauds, claimants, and imposters filtered through all of his writing. As a literary persona, Mark Twain railed against the pretension and stifling conventions of the dominant culture of his times. Clemens, the man, lived the greater part of his later years in the guise of an eastern literary gentleman, embodying the very values that his authorial identity satirized. He was a southerner living in the North; at home with the western frontiersman while playing the role of eastern gentleman; he wrote fervently on the materialistic, empty culture of the Gilded Age while living in one of the most garish homes in Hartford, Connecticut, and aspiring to great wealth through the different manifestations of get-rich-quick fever that overtook him at different times in his life.

Mark Twain's very earliest stories and characters, long before his marriage to the genteel Olivia Langdon, were a scathing indictment of the life and values that he, at least some of the time, seemed to embrace with great happiness during his married life. From the earliest days of his writing career through his invention of characters and pen names to flout conventional values and the establishment, he sought to create a distance between these strong views and his personal quest for respectability. At best, there existed an uneasy alliance between his life and his opinions. According to biographer Andrews, at Twain's height of fame, popularity, and wealth, while settled into family life in the early 1880s, there was a brief reconciliation of the man and his authorial identity, which was reflected in the text of *The Prince and the Pauper.* Later in that decade, as his fortunes declined and necessitated the move to Europe, Twain's deterministic philosophy became more evident and was reflected in the growing pessimism of his works.

Critic Everett Emerson suggests that Twain was never completely comfortable with his eastern life. Even as he read books on English history while preparing to write *The Prince and the Pauper,* he came across a host of crude and indelicate speech patterns that were permissible in the time of the Tudors. He wrote a satirical piece called "Conversation as It Was by the Fireside in the Time of the Tudors" and sent it anonymously to a new editor, who declined it with disgust. From all accounts Twain did not dare show it to Livy. In this way, Emerson suggests, Twain sought to release himself from a sense of being manacled by his daily life. Even in *The Prince and the Pauper*, which came closest to conforming to an established literary form, critics assert that Twain's irrepressible persona could not be completely disguised. Satirical pieces on the royal conventions and humorous plot twists have been cited as evidence of this.

THE IMPACT OF DUALITY ON HIS LITERATURE

Much debate has centered on a judgment of the impact of this dual life or the extent of Samuel Clemens's compromise insofar as it affected the literary output of Mark Twain. In 1920 critic Van Wyck Brooks brought out a scathing indictment of Twain as a genius thwarted by the genteel influences and swayed away from his natural and more authentic inclinations. Likewise, critic James Cox said *The Prince and the Pauper*, written with the encouragement and approval of Twain's immediate environment, was a betrayal of his true genius. On the other hand, in 1928 critic Fred Lewis Patee said Twain's literary friends did him a great service in pointing out where his real distinction lay, helping curb some of his inclinations to drift and write below the levels of his best work. "To assert that his marriage and his New England circle of friends were the Delilah sheers that robbed him of the full of his native powers is the veriest nonsense,"[47] said Patee. The most complete response to the Brooks thesis came from Bernard DeVoto in *Mark Twain's America*, published in 1932. DeVoto claimed that Livy, Howells, and others edited the form but not the substance of his work and that Twain was the first writer of truly American literature.

TWAIN'S STRENGTHS AND LIMITATIONS

In 1835, the year Mark Twain was born, Alexis de Tocqueville published the first part of his famous study *Democracy in America*, in which he predicted the rise of a new type of literature, a literature of democracy. This would not "exhibit the order, regularity, skill and art of aristocratic literature," he said, but rather a "rude and untutored vigor" striving more "to astonish than to please and to stir passions than to charm taste."[48] Mark Twain was the embodiment of these predictions. He lived the life of the American people, and he elevated the local dialects, values, and common sense into a national literature. His love of the river, of an unspoiled frontier, spoke to the national psyche.

And yet through his life and work the man and his authorial identity continued to strive for respectability and for recognition in the context of the British European literary tradition. He proclaimed America the greatest country on Earth and yet perceived his honorary degree from Britain's Oxford University as the ultimate acknowledgement of his stature. He compared himself to such figures as Charles Dickens and William Makepeace Thackeray. Even as the embodiment of the ultimate American symbol of defiance and autonomy, Twain chose to withhold many of his deepest convictions from public scrutiny in deference to prevailing opinions. His "profound intellectual timorousness, his abiding fear of his own ideas, his incurable cowardice in the face of public disapproval,"[49] was how H.L. Mencken described these limitations.

The tragedy of the author was his inability to accept and sit securely in his greatness, in the place that his unique and unconventional American literature had in the context of world literature. Twain was never completely convinced of his literary stature. He reportedly felt like an imposter both in his chosen vocation and in his life. This theme ran through much of his writing. The tragedy of the man was his inability to reach some inner accord in later life. In *The Prince and the Pauper* the courtiers around Tom Canty could not understand his assertion that he was an impostor, that he denied his exalted identity. He had a humble background, but in his brief reign he demonstrated wisdom and compassion beyond the reigning monarchs of the day. Both his betrayal of his mother and his crippling conscience and reversal made him an endearing and very real character. It gave him that real human dimension that was Twain's strongest suit. In the character of Tom Canty, Mark Twain was writing his own story.

For all of the contradictions of his life, the very human limitations of the man, and his personal despair in later years, Mark Twain always laughed, amused, and found a lighter, more absurd side to life until the end. He opened peoples' eyes to injustice, oppression, hypocrisy, and their own foibles by making them laugh. He broached a common humanity that strides across barriers of all sorts and speaks to a basic human need for freedom, independence, and a spiritual frontier embodied in the raft floating down the great Mississippi River. Twain brought the romance of a wide-open, unspoiled country alive in his literature. His books maintain it. Couched in the idylls of a childhood long gone, Mark Twain's greatest works offered readers in the flurry of change and turmoil during the nineteenth century a respite, a haven, a refuge, harking back to simpler times. A century later they have the same magic.

NOTES

1. Quoted in Louis J. Budd, *Critical Essays on Mark Twain, 1910–1980.* Boston: G.K. Hall, 1983, p. 43.
2. Quoted in Milton Meltzer, *Mark Twain Himself.* New York: Wings Books, 1960, p. 1.
3. Quoted in John Lauber, *The Making of Mark Twain.* New York: American Heritage, 1985, p. 12.
4. Quoted in Lauber, *The Making of Mark Twain,* p. 13.
5. Lauber, *The Making of Mark Twain,* p. 31.
6. Quoted in Lauber, *The Making of Mark Twain,* p. 14.
7. Quoted in Lauber, *The Making of Mark Twain,* p 14.
8. Quoted in Katie de Koster, ed., *Readings on Mark Twain.* San Diego: Greenhaven, 1996, p. 16.
9. Quoted in Lauber, *The Making of Mark Twain,* p. 22.
10. Lauber, *The Making of Mark Twain,* p. 22.
11. Quoted in Lauber, *The Making of Mark Twain,* p. 23.
12. Quoted in Everett Emerson, *Mark Twain: A Literary Life.* Philadelphia: University of Pennsylvania Press, 2000, p. 2.
13. Quoted in Meltzer, *Mark Twain Himself,* p. 17.
14. Quoted in de Koster, *Readings on Mark Twain,* p. 17.
15. Quoted in de Koster, *Readings on Mark Twain,* p. 18.
16. A.B. Paine, *Mark Twain: A Biography. The Personal and Literary Life of Samuel Langhorne Clemens.* New York: Harper and Brothers, 1912, p. 75.
17. Paine, *Mark Twain,* p. 82.
18. Emerson, *Mark Twain,* p. 4.
19. Quoted in Emerson, *Mark Twain,* p. 4.
20. Quoted in Emerson, *Mark Twain,* p. 32.
21. Quoted in Paine, *Mark Twain,* p. 126.
22. Quoted in Lauber, *The Making of Mark Twain,* p. 65.

23. Quoted in Meltzer, *Mark Twain Himself,* p. 43.
24. Quoted in Meltzer, *Mark Twain Himself,* p. 43.
25. Paine, *Mark Twain,* p. 178.
26. Paine, *Mark Twain,* p. 182.
27. Quoted in de Koster, *Readings on Mark Twain,* p. 30.
28. Paine, *Mark Twain,* p. 219.
29. Quoted in Emerson, *Mark Twain,* p. 20.
30. Emerson, *Mark Twain,* p. 21.
31. Emerson, *Mark Twain,* p. 17.
32. Emerson, *Mark Twain,* p. 36.
33. Quoted in Emerson, *Mark Twain,* p. 36.
34. Emerson, *Mark Twain,* p. 36.
35. Quoted in Emerson, *Mark Twain,* p. 45.
36. Quoted in Emerson, *Mark Twain,* p. 49.
37. Paine, *Mark Twain,* p. 354.
38. Quoted in Emerson, *Mark Twain,* p. 58.
39. Quoted in Meltzer, *Mark Twain Himself,* p. 123.
40. Quoted in Meltzer, *Mark Twain Himself,* p. 123.
41. Joe Fulton, *Mark Twain's Ethical Realism.* Columbia: University of Missouri Press, 1997, p. 1.
42. Quoted in Kenneth Andrews, *Nook Farm: Mark Twain's Hartford Circle.* Cambridge, MA: Harvard University Press, 1950, p. 83.
43. Andrews, *Nook Farm,* p. 83.
44. Quoted in Andrews, *Nook Farm,* p. 124.
45. Andrews, *Nook Farm,* p. 215.
46. Quoted in de Koster, *Readings on Mark Twain,* p. 42.
47. Quoted in Budd, *Critical Essays on Mark Twain, 1910–1980,* p. 78.
48. Quoted in de Koster, *Readings on Mark Twain,* p. 47.
49. Quoted in Budd, *Critical Essays on Mark Twain, 1910–1980,* p. 46.

Characters and Plot

Major Characters

Tom Canty: Tom Canty is a fourteen-year-old boy born to John Canty and his wife in the 1530s in England. The family lives in poverty and squalor in a crowded room in Offal Court in the backstreets of London. From a young age, Tom is forced to beg for food by his merciless and brutish father. Tom suffers beatings from his father when he comes home empty-handed, but he accepts this treatment because it is all that he has ever known.

Tom is an unusual boy in many respects. For example, he takes an interest in learning classical languages and history from a kindly old priest and neighbor, Father Andrew. He has a lively imagination and dreams of living in royal surroundings and giving orders to those around him. With a wisdom beyond his years, Tom commands a lot of respect from the poor folk who come and ask his advice in local disputes. He is considered a hero by all who know him, with the exception of his family.

Tom trades places with Prince Edward and assumes his identity for most of the book. At first he denies he is the prince and is thought to be mad by the members of the royal court. Though he is initially intimidated by the demands of his new position, as the novel progresses he becomes more accustomed to the royal treatment. He brings the same native intelligence, compassion, and sound judgment to a number of cases in which his subjects have been accused of serious crimes based on scanty evidence. He is hailed as a champion of the oppressed.

Tom becomes so enamored of his new lifestyle that he manages to put his concern for the fate of the real Edward out of his mind. He even denies knowing his mother when she recognizes him in the coronation procession. This slowly dawning corruption of his character is quickly reversed when Tom becomes overwhelmed with shame and guilt at his betrayal of his loving mother. Tom readily concurs when the real Edward bursts into the proceedings and declares him an imposter. He is rewarded for his honesty by being made a director of Christ's Hospital for poor boys. Tom lives to a ripe old age. As a white-haired elderly man, he is admired and respected by all who know him.

Prince Edward: Prince Edward is the first son of Henry VIII and heir to the throne of England. In voice, manner, and physical appearance, he bears an uncanny resemblance to the pauper, Tom Canty. When the prince is mistakenly thrown into Tom Canty's life, he continuously protests and declares himself of noble birth. This leads to beatings by John Canty and mockery by his ruffian companions. Like Tom, he is thought insane by those around him, who believe he is suffering from delusions. He ignores all the rejection and humiliation and maintains that he is the real prince throughout the novel.

Edward demonstrates a strong sense of compassion from the very beginning. The central action of the book involves his education about the impact of some of the harsh and unjust laws of his land. Edward grows and matures as he sees terrible injustice and cruelty resulting from the implementation of the king's laws. He vows to make amends when he becomes king. True to this promise, Edward becomes known as an unusually merciful ruler for those times. He dies at a young age.

Miles Hendon: Miles Hendon plays the role of chief protector of young Edward when he is cast out into the rabble of London. Although he does not believe the boy's assertions about his regal status, Miles becomes very fond of Edward and vows to be his guardian. Miles is a former soldier and adventurer and has just returned home from a war overseas. He was originally sent off to war because of his wicked younger brother Hugh's false assertions that he planned to elope with the Lady Edith. Though Miles did indeed love his cousin Edith, she was pledged in marriage to his older brother Arthur, and Miles respected the union. Still, Hugh's charge got attention and Miles was quickly sent off to European battlefields. There, Miles was captured and imprisoned for seven years. When he finally returns home, Miles finds his father and older brother dead and the Lady Edith married to Hugh. When they meet, Hugh declares that Miles is an imposter and forces the Lady Edith to do likewise. Miles is once again banished from his home. His true identity is established by Edward when he regains the throne. Hugh is then banished to Europe, where he dies, leaving Miles to wed the lovely Lady Edith.

MINOR CHARACTERS

John Canty: John Canty, Tom's father, is a beggar and thief. Like his mother, Gammer Canty (who lives with Tom's family), he drinks heavily, and regularly beats his wife and children. He has no redeeming qualities. After murdering Father Andrew, he flees Offal Court and pursues Edward (thought to be Tom) to force him to beg for him. He organizes a gang of thieves and ruffians, which includes his sidekick, Hugo. Hugo is a thug who takes great delight in making young Edward's life miserable. In his last major appearance, John Canty is opposed by Miles Hendon, who rescues Edward from his clutches. John Canty flees and is never heard of again.

Mrs. Canty: Tom's mother is a simple woman who lives under the thumb of her cruel husband and mother-in-law. She is loving, kind, and gentle with her children and secretly brings Tom food in defiance of her husband's orders. Her main role is in acting as a catalyst for her son's betrayal and crippling guilty conscience. This occurs when Tom denies knowing her when she cries out to him in the coronation procession. Her twin daughters, Tom's fifteen-year-old sisters, Bet and Nan, are cast in her same mold.

Hugh Hendon: Hugh Hendon is Miles's younger brother and favorite of their father Richard. He plots and schemes with evil intent throughout his life. He marries Lady Edith for her substantial income. After forging a note declaring that Miles was killed in action, he inherits his family's estate. When Edward is reinstated as king, Hugh is stripped of his false status and banished to Europe. He dies, leaving the Lady Edith free to marry her beloved Miles.

Henry VIII: Henry VIII, king of England, is on his deathbed at the opening of the novel. Although not known for being a merciful ruler, he is gentle with his young son Edward. When Tom is mistaken for Edward and denies this identity, Henry feels very grieved at what he believes is his son's mental affliction. He does acknowledge Edward's compassionate nature in an affectionate manner when he sees Tom exhibit similar traits.

The Mad Hermit: Edward encounters the hermit's house in the woods while fleeing from John Canty. The hermit is a thin old man with a long white beard. He is a recluse who has denounced all worldly associations and is under the delusion that he is an archangel. He believes he would have been made pope if the king hadn't disbanded his monastery. By putting on a gentle front, he lulls Edward into a false sense of security. While the boy sleeps, he ties him up and prepares to stab him with a knife to avenge the king's actions. His evil scheme is interrupted by the arrival of Miles Hendon.

PLOT SUMMARY

The Prince and the Pauper is set in England in the sixteenth century. The main action of the novel begins at 9:00 A.M. on January 27, 1547, seventeen and a half hours before the death of Henry VIII. The main action of the novel covers the period until the crowning of Edward as king on February 20.

THE BIRTH OF THE PRINCE AND THE PAUPER

On a memorable fall day in 1533, all of the loyal English subjects rejoice at the birth of Edward, Prince of Wales, the first male heir of King Henry VIII. On the very same day, in a hovel in the backstreets of London, the Canty family feels distress when their son Tom is born. Another child means another mouth to feed in the already overcrowded one-room household of John Canty, his mother, his wife, and their one-year-old twin daughters, Bet and Nan.

TOM'S EARLY LIFE

Fourteen years pass. Like many of the poor in London at the time, the Canty household survives by begging and stealing. From a young age, Tom is forced to beg for food and suffers harsh punishment from his cruel father if he returns home empty-handed. Unlike the other poor boys in Offal Court, Tom becomes literate thanks to the devoted teaching of Father Andrew, an elderly priest who lives in his building. Father Andrew was reduced to living on a pittance when his church was disbanded by the king's decree. This was one of many examples of the religious intolerance that characterized Henry VIII's reign.

From the worlds that open up to him from reading books, Tom develops a vibrant imaginative life. He puts aside the thought of his aches and pains from his father's floggings by dreaming of the royal court, and he fantasizes about one day meeting a real prince. Over time, he begins to speak, act, and even feel like a prince while playing with his companions in Offal Court. His fantasy world among lords and ladies become so real to him that when he awakens from his nightly dreams in their sordid one-room hovel, he feels heartbreak and bitterness.

TOM MEETS THE PRINCE

In keeping with his greatest wish, Tom goes to the royal palace and glimpses the young and finely clad prince in the courtyard. As he presses his face against the bars, he is pushed roughly away by the king's sentinel. Young Edward sees this display and is overcome with compassion for the young pauper. He orders his sentry to admit Tom Canty. The prince takes Tom to his chambers and begins to inquire about Tom's life. Although the prince is shocked by the cruelty of Tom's father and grandmother, he is fascinated by Tom's freedom to dance and sing with his friends in Offal Court. This touches a real longing inside the prince to be free from his palace life. For a lark, the boys decide to exchange clothes. They are struck by their strong physical likeness. The prince notices that Tom's arm has been bruised from the rough treatment by his guard, and fuming with anger he goes out to chastise his servant. On his way out of the royal chamber, he takes time to conceal an important (but yet unrevealed) object in a special hiding place. When he comes upon the guard, he is mistaken for the beggar boy and is hurled out into the crowd. Young Edward protests wildly but is mocked and ridiculed by his subjects.

EDWARD'S TROUBLES BEGIN

Jostled by the mob, Edward finds himself among the inmates of Christ's Hospital, a home for poor boys. They laugh and jeer at him, but Edward pities their plight. He secretly resolves to make sure that the boys are given the chance to become educated when he regains the throne. He sets out to find Tom's family in Offal Court, convinced that they will help him clear up the question of his true identity. John Canty catches sight of him and drags him off, swearing and cursing amid Prince Edward's protests.

TOM'S PROBLEMS AS THE PRINCE

Tom is a little disturbed at the prince's long absence. Eventually members of the court spot Tom loitering. Bearing such a close resemblance, however, he is believed to be the prince. He protests that he is just poor Tom Canty, a pauper from Offal Court. The king and the royal court believe that the young prince has gone insane. Yet when the king asks him a question in Latin, thanks to Father Andrew's good teachings, Tom can answer. From this the king concludes that though his son is mad, it is only a temporary condition. As the king lies ill on his deathbed, Tom hears his talk of the planned execution of the duke of Norfolk, who awaits in the tower. Tom expresses grief at this notion. From this display, Henry feels reassured that the boy really is his son, for it is in Edward's nature to feel such compassion.

Tom makes many blunders in his new role as prince. Edward's uncle quietly instructs him in how to uphold his princely dignity. He enjoys the company of Edward's sister Elizabeth and cousin Lady Jane Grey, who are gentle and forgiving of his unusual behavior. In secret, the king's advisers are most perplexed. They believe that, though it is likely that a pauper would masquerade as a prince, it is most odd that a prince would declare himself a beggar. They are all the more concerned since the death of Henry VIII is imminent.

EDWARD'S TRIALS AS A PAUPER

Among the Canty family, Edward's assertions about his true identity are taken as evidence that he too has gone insane. John Canty's response is to try to beat some sense into him. Tom's mother and sisters, however, are kind to Edward. Still, Tom's mother is struck by something different about the boy who is supposed to be her son. She decides to put him to a test. When Tom is awakened from sleep, he characteristically places his hand, palm turned outward, against his face. The boy fails this test twice, and Tom's mother remains perplexed.

Meanwhile, John Canty is warned that he is being pursued for the murder of Father Andrew. Angered by the good priest's kindness to his son, Canty, in a drunken fit, had struck him a death blow. The family flees. In the ruckus, Edward escapes and goes to London Bridge. He concludes that Tom Canty has usurped his position as prince and must be hanged for this treasonous act.

THE DEATH OF HENRY VIII

When Henry VIII dies, Tom's first act is to show mercy to the duke of Norfolk and give him his freedom. Tom declares that the king's law should be one of mercy and not of bloodshed.

Meanwhile, Edward learns with great sadness of his father's passing. Under London Bridge, he is captured again by John Canty, but rescued by Miles Hendon, a passing and chivalrous soldier, who intervenes to stop Canty's cruel treatment of his supposed son. Miles listens to Edward's assertions about his true identity. Though he gives them no credence, he feels a fondness for the young lad and decides to humor him and take him under his wing.

Miles explains his own circumstances. His mother died when he was a boy. His father, Richard, was blind to the faults of his younger brother Hugh, who is vicious and underhanded. Hugh accused Miles of planning to elope with the lovely Lady Edith, his cousin, who was promised in marriage to Arthur, the eldest Hendon boy. Richard believed some false evidence that was planted by the conniving Hugh and banished Miles to fight in the wars of Europe for three years. While at war, Miles was captured and imprisoned for seven years. He has just escaped and is making his way back to Hendon Hall to rejoin his family.

Edward tells Miles his story, which Miles does not believe. In gratitude for Miles's rescue from John Canty, Edward dubs him a knight. Miles humors the boy, still unconvinced that he is the heir to England's throne. Miles goes to sleep outside the room at the inn, where they pause to rest for the night. When he goes in the next morning to awaken Edward, he finds to his horror that the boy is gone.

TOM AS KING

When Tom awakens, he is surprised to find himself still a captive and a king. Part of him yearns for his freedom on the backstreets of London with his boisterous companions. He finds the affairs of state onerous, and the days are heavy listening to the business of the court. He meets Humphrey Marlow, his twelve-year-old whipping boy. Humphrey's job is to be whipped for any of the prince's transgressions. Tom realizes that he can take advantage of Humphrey's knowledge of the royal court and gleans much useful information from their conversations.

Tom begins to adjudicate some of the cases brought to trial. One man has been accused of poisoning another based on very scanty evidence. Tom is shocked to learn that his punishment is to be boiled alive. He declares that henceforth no such cruel punishments are to be given to his subjects. He uses his common sense to adjudicate other accusations and thus wins the respect of the court for his fine powers of reasoning and deduction. These are the same skills that the poor folk in Offal Court once acknowledged. At a sumptuous state dinner with all of the lords and ladies of the court, Tom performs credibly as prince and is beginning to feel at home among all the pomp and pageantry.

THE PRINCE ENCOUNTERS TRAMPS, PEASANTS, AND THE MAD HERMIT

Meanwhile, John Canty has discovered Edward's where-abouts and through trickery lures him away from Miles's protection. He has changed his name to John Hobbs to escape capture and has joined up with his gang of twenty-five thieves, including a particularly villainous thug called Hugo. Edward continues to maintain that he is the real king of England even among this gang of ruffians. They anoint him "Foo Foo the First, King of the Mooncalves." He bears these insults with a steely gaze, and quiet tears of shame and indignation.

Among the rowdy crowd, Edward hears some of the stories of once-innocent peasants who have lost their families because of the harsh penalties imposed by English law. One man's mother was burnt as a witch after a patient she nursed had died. His wife died after she received repeated lashings as punishment for begging for food. His children died of starvation. This same man lost an ear in the stocks and was finally branded with a large "S" as a symbol for slave. He was in hiding from his master after fleeing cruel treatment. Edward is shocked and expresses horror at the severity of these punishments. He vows to end such laws.

John Canty tries to force Edward to beg for him. The boy escapes from Canty, and after approaching several farms and being forcefully ejected, finds refuge in a barn. Here he is given comfort by a calf who snuggles next to him for the night. Edward has been treated so roughly for so long by his own kind that the young king finds great solace in his new company. In the morning, two peasant girls discover him. He tells them his story and they are the first to believe him. Edward is very grateful. Their mother is kind and generous and gives him food. She concludes that he is a kitchenhand and sets him to work helping with the chores. When Edward overhears John Canty at the door, he flees into the woods.

As the twilight hours approach, Edward is cold, lonely, and hungry. He glimpses a light in the window of a small house. Peeking through the window, he sees an old man praying. Delighted to have stumbled upon a holy hermit, he knocks at the door. The old man seems to believe Edward's story, for which he is most relieved. But as their talk progresses, the hermit declares that he is an archangel. He also says that he was destined to be the pope, but the king intervened. Edward becomes concerned that the hermit is demented, yet decides to accept his offer of food and a soft bed. As Edward sleeps, the hermit becomes enraged by the king's actions in thwarting his ambitions; he ties up the young boy and begins to sharpen a large knife, preparing to kill him. At the critical moment, Miles Hendon knocks at the door. The hermit tells him the boy has left and they both take off after him, the hermit secretly planning to return and complete his mission. Edward listens to their retreating footsteps with a sinking heart. John Canty and his rogue companion Hugo turn up and discover the boy. They untie him and cart him off with them.

EDWARD AS PRISONER

Edward spends several miserable days moving about with John Canty's gang of thieves. Hugo takes a particular dislike to the boy's airs and graces and frames him for stealing a pig from a passing woman. As the crowd gathers about the boy-called-thief, Miles Hendon comes yet again to his rescue. He persuades the people that justice must be done and the boy should be brought before the law.

Edward is startled to discover that the penalty for stealing a pig of such worth is hanging. The peasant woman is horrified that the young lad might suffer such a punishment. She declares the value of the pig to be much lower to circumvent such a harsh outcome. The king and Miles escape while being led off to prison.

MILES HENDON DISOWNED

The two companions travel happily toward Hendon Hall. "Embrace me!" declares Miles when he first sees his brother

Hugh. But Hugh draws back and claims that his brother Miles is dead and that this man is an imposter. Miles finds out that his father and elder brother have died and that his beloved Lady Edith is Hugh's wife. Miles and Edward are taken to prison, where a number of witnesses under duress confirm that Miles is an imposter. Even the Lady Edith says she does not know him. But she does warn the two prisoners that Hugh is a merciless tyrant and that they must escape his clutches.

While in prison, Edward is comforted by two women whose sole crime is that they are Baptists, a religion not tolerated by the state. Edward watches with horror as these kind women are burned at the stake. Overcome with grief, their daughters try to fling themselves on the mounting flames. Another woman who was guilty of stealing a yard of cloth is to be hanged. Edward acknowledges the injustice, vowing to show mercy as regent.

Miles Hendon is sentenced to the humiliation of being locked in the stocks at the town square. People mock, insult, and throw eggs at him. When Edward objects to this treatment, he is sentenced to lashes of the whip. Miles steps in and offers to take the young boy's punishment. Hugh gladly obliges and increases the whipping to twelve lashes. Miles bears the heavy blows with equanimity. Edward expresses his heartfelt gratitude and dubs Miles an earl. Miles resolves to go to London to plead his case before the king.

TOM CANTY ENJOYS HIS ROYAL STATUS

Tom Canty, meanwhile, has lost all his misgivings about his new position and has become accustomed to the royal treatment. Though he remains a champion of the oppressed, he begins to find that his four hundred servants are too few and triples their number. Tom had been concerned about the plight of the real king, but over time he has pushed these thoughts out of his mind. When they do arise, he feels guilt and shame. He has also succeeded in putting his mother and sisters out of his thoughts most of the time. And yet when their poverty and suffering crosses his mind, he feels remorse.

CORONATION DAY

On February 20, 1547, the young prince is to be crowned king of England. As Tom rides proudly through the streets for the procession to Westminster Abbey, he waves at his loyal subjects and throws gold coins to the crowds. He is intoxicated with his great status in the land. But much to his horror, he catches sight of a pale and distressed face peering at him. It is his mother. Tom's palm flies upward to his face, the old involuntary gesture his mother knows so well. She cries out to her darling child. Tom, however, declares that he doesn't know her. As she is pushed rudely away by his guards, great shame falls upon him. Royalty loses all its glamour. Unable to contain his emotions, Tom cries out that the woman is indeed his mother. His royal courtiers are alarmed by what they see as their king's reversion to his insane delusions.

The coronation proceedings continue. Just as the archbishop is about to crown young Tom king of England, Edward bursts into the hall and declares "I am the true king!" As his servants rush to remove the poorly clad boy, Tom intervenes and admits the deception. The crowd is bewildered. They look from one boy to the other and notice their remarkable resemblance. The lord protector asks Edward many questions about the court, and though Edward answers them all correctly, he is still not convinced of his identity. Finally he asks Edward about the great seal that had been missing since before Henry had died. Edward tells them of its hiding place in his chamber. But alas his courtier returns without the seal. Tom asks him to think carefully and retrace the exact details of the very first day of their exchange. Edward recalls moving the seal to a special hiding place as he left Tom alone in his chamber to chastise the guard. The seal is recovered and Edward is declared the real king. Tom embarrassingly admits that, unsure of its purpose, he has used the great seal to crack nuts. The whole court erupts in laughter.

Miles Hendon arrives at the court and is stunned to find his young companion on the royal throne. Edward restores Miles to his rightful title and banishes his wicked brother Hugh from England. Edward learns of Tom's merciful acts as king and praises him. He declares that Tom should be governor of Christ's Hospital for boys and that all therein should be educated and amply provided for. Tom is given a special dress suitable to a man of the court so that all who view him will recall his royal days.

JUSTICE FOR ALL

Later, it is revealed that Lady Edith was threatened that if she confirmed Miles's true identity, he would be slaughtered. Still she refuses to testify against Hugh when the king decides his punishment. Suffering his banishment, however, Hugh is sent to Europe, where he soon dies. Miles, now earl of Kent, marries Edith. John Canty is never heard from again. Edward frees many of the people he met in the prisons accused of petty crimes. He also provides good homes for the daughters of the kind women he saw burnt at the stake. Young Edward never tires of telling his stories as a wandering pauper. This continually replenishes his heart with goodness and mercy. Though cut short by his untimely death, his rule is hailed as a merciful one for those times. Tom Canty and Miles Hendon are favorites of the king and deeply mourn his passing.

CHAPTER 1

Origins and Context

READINGS ON
THE PRINCE AND THE PAUPER

How the Novel Came to Be Written

Albert Bigelow Paine

Albert Bigelow Paine, Twain's chosen biographer, published *Mark Twain: A Biography* in 1912, based on his long and close association with Samuel Clemens. In the following article, published in *The Mentor* in 1928, Paine reports his discussions with Twain, who said he first conceived of writing *The Prince and the Pauper* after reading Charlotte Yonge's *The Prince and the Page* in 1877. However, Paine suggests that Twain's extensive reading of British history and fascination with Elizabethan England and the century preceding her rule, were clear influences on the inception of the novel. He says Mark Twain's main purpose in writing *The Prince and the Pauper* was to protest injustice and abuses of authority, a theme central to much of his fiction. In this case his concern was to point to the cruel and severe punishments inflicted for minor crimes in the reign of Henry VIII. Paine describes both the pleasure of the author in preparing the book and the unusual approval of his wife Livy, who showed clear preference for this work over the other novel in preparation at the time, *The Adventures of Huckleberry Finn*. Paine's biography is still considered a major source of information on the author's life, while being generally regarded as biased in its uncritical praise of Mark Twain.

Even the author himself can never be quite sure in tracing a tale to its definite origin, its ultimate source. Once when I asked Mark Twain if he could remember the genesis of certain of his stories he said:

> I remember some of them very well. *Joan of Arc* had its beginning almost in my childhood when one day I picked up a stray leaf from some old book about her, blown along the

Excerpted from "*The Prince and the Pauper:* How Mark Twain Came to Write the Story in Which He Himself Took Such Keen Delight," by Albert Bigelow Paine, *The Mentor*, December 1928.

street by the wind; the *Connecticut Yankee* idea came while I
was reading a book of Sir Thomas Mallory's stories given me
by George W. Cable; I began writing the *Prince and the Pauper* after reading a little book I found in my sister-in-law's library at Elmira.

That the story of *The Prince and the Pauper* began there is
certain. But Mark Twain had always been a reader of romantic history, and it may be that long years before he wrote
the first page of that immortal story of Tom Canty of Offal
Court, who became prince and king while the real prince
was being buffeted about as a ragged outcast, he had read
the legend of King Robert of Sicily and unconsciously had
stored away the moral and the situation for future use.

One day in 1877 he picked up at Elmira a little story of England in the thirteenth century, written by Charlotte M.
Yonge and entitled *The Prince and the Page,* which told of a
prince who studied the world at close range by living for a
period of years disguised as a blind beggar. In a flash his
story came. Not only would he disguise a prince as a beggar
but also a beggar as a prince. He would have them exchange
places in the world, in order that each might learn the burdens of the other's life and thereby be moved to a broader
tolerance and understanding.

HOW THE PLOT EVOLVED

It was a typical Mark Twain plot, in a setting that appealed
strongly to his imagination. His mind was richly stored with
reading of Elizabethan England and the century that preceded the reign of the Virgin Queen. In old volumes he had
read with hot resentment of the excesses and cruelties of
primitive punishment of petty offenders, and even innocent
men and women and children, being subjected to hanging
and boiling in oil. He could not himself ride forth, a St. George,
to slay the dragon of injustice; but in imagination he could
send out his two little heroes to battle valiantly for the right.

The development of the tale naturally brought many problems. His first idea was to use the late King Edward VII (then
Prince of Wales) at about fifteen as one of his two heroes. But
that would have been too close to our own time to make it
seem plausible, so he followed back through history until he
came to the little son of Henry VIII who reigned briefly as Edward VI. Then arose the question of how to effect the change
in station. The old device of changelings in the cradle (later

used in *Pudd'nhead Wilson*) presented itself to him but it could not provide the situations he had in mind. Finally he found the solution in the playful interchange of raiment and the startling and unexpected result. His first idea had been to make a play. He visualized the gorgeous background of the age, with its colorful costuming. But in his mind *The Prince and the Pauper* was molding itself as a story. Very well, as a story it should be written. He could dramatize it later.

Of all Mark Twain's stories none brought him greater joy in the writing than *The Prince and the Pauper*, despite the fact that after beginning it and writing four hundred manuscript pages he put it aside for other work and did not take it up again for more than two years. Then he returned to it with fresh ardor. Every afternoon or evening, when he had finished his chapter, he gathered his children about him and read to them what he had written, drawing new inspiration for the morrow from their keen enjoyment. He told William Dean Howells that if he never sold a copy of *The Prince and the Pauper* his jubilant delight in writing it would suffer no diminution. Later he wrote to Mr. Howells: "I take so much pleasure in my story I am loath to hurry, not wanting to get it done. Did I ever tell you the plot of it? It begins at 9 A.M., January 27, 1547."

Then he went on to give a detailed synopsis of his plot, which by this time he had worked out with unusual completeness, and illustrated its underlying motive:

> My idea is to afford a realizing sense of the exceeding severity of the laws of that day by inflicting some of their penalties upon the king himself, and allowing him a chance to see the rest of them applied to others; all of which is to account for certain mildnesses which distinguish Edward VI's reign from those that precede it and follow it.

He adds jubilantly:

> Imagine this fact: I have even fascinated Mrs. Clemens with this yarn for youth. My stuff generally gets considerable damning with faint praise out of her, but this time it is all the other way. She is become the horse-leech's daughter and my mill doesn't grind fast enough for her. This is no mean triumph, my dear sir.

TWO BOOKS OR ONE

The Prince and the Pauper was first published in 1881. Near the end of the preceding year Mark Twain had written to his sister regarding two stories which, according to a verbal un-

SUSY CLEMENS ON *THE PRINCE AND THE PAUPER*
Susy Clemens, Twain's middle daughter, shared her mother's enthusiasm for The Prince and the Pauper. *In the following excerpt from* Papa: An Intimate Biography of Mark Twain *written when she was thirteen, Susy says her father's more serious and sympathetic nature was evident in the novel, amidst his inevitable humor.*

One of papa's latest books is *The Prince and the Pauper* and it is unquestionably the best book he has ever written, some people want him to keep to his old style, some gentleman wrote him, "I enjoyed Huckleberry Finn immensely and am glad to see that you have returned to your old style." That enoyed me that enoyed me greatly, because it trobles me to have so few people know papa, I mean realy know him, they think of Mark Twain as a humorist joking at everything; "And with a mop of reddish brown hair which sorely needs the barbars brush a roman nose, short stubby mustache, a sad care-worn face, with maney crow's feet" etc. That is the way people picture papa, I have wanted papa to write a book that would reveal something of his kind sympathetic nature, and *The Prince and the Pauper* partly does it. The book is full of lovely charming ideas, and oh the language! It is *perfect.* I think that one of the most touching scenes in it, is where the pauper is riding on horseback with his nobles in the "recognition procession" and he sees his mother oh and then what followed! How she runs to his side, when she sees him throw up his hand palm outward, and is rudely pushed off by one of the King's officers, and then how the little pauper's conscience troubles him when he remembers the shameful words that were falling from his lips, when she was turned from his side "I know you not woman" and how his grandeurs were stricken valueless, and his pride consumed to ashes. It is a wonderfully beautiful and touching little scene, and papa has described it so wonderfully. I never saw a man with so much variety of feeling as papa has; now the *The Prince and the Pauper* is full of touching places; but there is most always a streak of humor in them somewhere. Now in the coronation—in the stirring coronation, just after the little king has got his crown back again papa brings that in about the Seal, where the pauper says he used the Seal "to crack nuts with." Oh it is so funny and nice! Papa very seldom writes a passage without some humor in it somewhere, and I dont think he ever will.

Susy Clemens, *Papa: An Intimate Biography of Mark Twain,* edited by Charles Neider, 1985.

derstanding with his publishers, were to go into one book, an arrangement which his wife did not endorse. One of the stories, the one on which Mark Twain set high store, was *The Prince and the Pauper.* The other, then unfinished and lightly regarded, was the tale that the world was to know as *The Adventures of Huckleberry Finn.* Eventually Mrs. Clemens had her way. As a book by itself, handsomely illustrated and finely bound, *The Prince and the Pauper* was published in England, Canada, Germany and the United States early in December, 1881.

In a letter written in 1880 to his sister Mark Twain tells of the situation as far as the two books he had just finished were concerned, and what his wife, "Livy," had to say about them:

> I have two stories, and by the verbal agreement they are both going into the same book; but Livy says they're not, and, by George the First, she ought to know. She says they're going into separate books, and that one of them is going to be elegantly gotten up, even if the elegance of it eats up the publisher's profits and mine too.
>
> I anticipate that publisher's melancholy surprise when he calls here Tuesday. However, let him suffer, it is his own fault. People who fix up agreements with me without first finding out what Livy's plans are take their fate into their own hands.
>
> I said *two* stories, but one of them is only half done; two or three months work on it yet. I shall tackle it Wednesday or Thursday; that is, if Livy yields and allows both stories to go in one book, which I hope she won't.

Although a success, it puzzled many readers, accustomed to looking for the joke in Mark Twain's work, and some reviewers went so far as to refer to it as one of Mark Twain's big jokes, meaning probably that he had created a chapter in English history with no foundation beyond his fancy. That was a surmise that Mark Twain had foreseen and feared. At one time he considered publishing *The Prince and the Pauper* anonymously, as later he did his *Joan of Arc,* in order to avert such a misunderstanding. There were hours immediately after the appearance of the book when he regretted that he had not done so.

DRAMATIZATION OF THE NOVEL

Of course in time *The Prince and the Pauper* became a play. The first production was by amateurs for the family and the neighbors, an adaptation of the story made by Mrs. Clemens, and presented in the Hartford home as a surprise party for

Mark Twain. There was one momentous hitch in that performance. The part of the prince was played by Olivia Susan Clemens, in childhood better known as Susy. There is a place where the prince says, "Fathers be alike, mayhap; mine hath not a doll's temper." The audience was quick to recognize the literal appropriateness of the utterance. It brought down the house.

On the professional stage *The Prince and the Pauper* made its first appearance in the autumn of 1889. The dramatization was made by Abby Sage Richardson, and Daniel Frohman secured Elsie Leslie, who, with Tommy Russell, had created the rôle of "Little Lord Fauntleroy," to take the double rôle of the prince and Tom Canty.

Opening at the Park Theater, Philadelphia, it proceeded to the Broadway Theater, New York. It was only relatively a success. The dual rôle was the handicap. With one performer playing both Tom Canty and the prince many of the strongest scenes had to be omitted. Mark Twain in vain urged the producers to find a second child actress. Certain legal complications added to the difficulty. The play had a distinguished revival on the night of November 19, 1907, when it was presented in the Children's Theater of the Jewish Educational Alliance, on the East Side of New York.

Nook Farm Writers and the Genteel Tradition

Kenneth R. Andrews

In *Nook Farm: Mark Twain's Hartford Circle*, Kenneth R. Andrews writes about the period of Twain's life from 1871 to 1891 in which he was close companions with a circle of writers and critics at Connecticut's Nook Farm. In the following excerpt from that book, Andrews describes how Nook Farm writers like Harriet Beecher Stowe (author of *Uncle Tom's Cabin*) urged Twain to write a "serious" novel that varied from his usual manner and style. Andrews counters the view that this advice stunted the growth of Twain's individuality and satiric genius during that period. Andrews believes the literary group accommodated Twain's "low brow" humor for they saw there was an underlying seriousness of purpose in his writing. Andrews suggests that even in the alien setting and atypical artistry of *The Prince and the Pauper* Mark Twain's irrepressible spirit shines through. The book was hailed by Nook Farm society as the pinnacle of Twain's literary achievements and they were dearly disappointed when his next book, *The Adventures of Huckleberry Finn*, was published.

It has often been said that the gentility of Hartford supposedly hostile to the burgeoning of Mark Twain's satiric power, helped warp him away from his mission as a satirist of his own times and imposed upon him a mediocre conventionality that emasculated his work and frustrated his spirit. The obvious untruth of such a judgment does not mean that Mark was unaffected by the standards of taste operative in Hartford and in [adjacent] Elmira. His conformity to those standards was for the most part an eager adaptation to the customs of Eastern culture. During the seventies and eight-

Reprinted with permission from the publisher from *Nook Farm: Mark Twain's Hartford Circle*, by Kenneth R. Andrews, pp. 188–99, Cambridge, MA: Harvard University Press. Copyright 1950 by the President and Fellows of Harvard College.

ies he was very much a member of his own generation. Its ideals were his own. . . . No conflict complicating his adjustment to the gentility of Hartford [is evident]. But he was most certainly the object of well-meaning advice that he go beyond the burlesque and realism (his stock in trade) and attempt the kind of book most highly regarded by gentlefolk.

Mark's encounter with practitioners of good taste outside his immediate family began in a meeting with Anson Burlingame [U.S. Ambassador to China], who urged him in Hawaii in 1866 to improve himself socially and culturally by associating only with his betters. Mrs. Fairbanks [a close confidante], who represented cultivated Cleveland, continued the course of instruction aboard the *Quaker City* in 1867. Olivia Langdon assumed responsibility for his tutelage upon their marriage in 1870 and thereafter welcomed the assistance of [eminent U.S. author, editor, and critic] William Dean Howells. All four of these advocates of good breeding, accepting more of Mark Twain's eccentricity and relative uncouthness than they attempted to modify, recommended chiefly that he discipline his inclination to burlesque in the direction of a graceful diction, a dignified literary personality, and a conscious regard for the polite conventions.

SOFTENING THE EDGES

A full realization of how much was accomplished, despite Mark's successful defense of his own individuality, requires the reading of his early sketches, which are frequently crude even by post-Victorian standards. A comparison of the *Alta* letters with *Innocents Abroad,* and of the Sacramento *Union* accounts of his Hawaiian trip with the relevant sections of *Roughing It,* shows many thoroughly sound revisions in favor of taste without a substantial dilution of vigor. A Mr. Brown, fictitious traveling companion who enabled Mark to be vulgar in his early travel letters without implicating himself, was eliminated altogether when the letters were revised for book publication. As Mark was settling into polite society, he excised much vulgarity, but by no means abandoned burlesque. In Hartford he could write and publish in spite of the disapproval of Livy and Howells "The Invalid's Story," a sketch in which the aroma of Limburger cheese, waxing potent in a heated baggage car, is mistaken for the smell of a corpse in a near-by coffin. Burlesque of this sort—the decay of corpses is a frequent reference in Mark's humor—became a permanent defect of his entire work. Its publication is evidence at least that whatever censorship he was subjected to was not really strict. From the perspective of our own time it often seems excessively tolerant.

EASTERN RESPONSE TO TWAIN

Mark Twain's humor, even in its earlier and cruder form, had, in fact, been enthusiastically received in Hartford. Before he moved to Nook Farm, his work had been discussed in the Monday Evening Club [an elite group which met to discuss topical issues], and praise of him in [the local newspaper] the *Courant* had been warm. As early as 1866 a newspaper of near-by Springfield, edited then by Samuel Bowles (the nationally respected liberal editor and close friend of [Nook Farm lawyer] John Hooker), had reprinted an estimate by a Western critic which represents Eastern opinion of his early writing.

> His humor is peculiar to himself; if of any type, it is rather of the western character of ludicrous exaggeration and audacious statement, which perhaps is more thoroughly national and American than even the Yankee delineations of [James Russell] Lowell [editor of *Atlantic Monthly*]. His humor has more motive than that of Artemus Ward [U.S. humorist 1834–67]; he is something of a satirist, although his satire is not always subtle or refined. He has shrewdness and a certain hearty abhorrence of shams which will make his faculty serviceable to mankind. His talent is so well based that he can write seriously and well when he chooses, which is perhaps the best test of true humor. His faults are crudeness, coarseness, and an occasional Panurge-like [mischievous] plainness of statement.

Bret Harte [U.S. author] wrote this early comment. Like later Hartford criticism, it dignified Mark's buffoonery with seriousness of purpose.

PRESSURE TO WRITE A "SERIOUS" NOVEL

But though Mark's friends in Hartford shared the general delight in *Innocents Abroad* and *Roughing It*, they began to request more and more explicitly that he rise above the limitations of humor to attempt a really serious book. They did not suggest a higher aspiration because they discredited his accomplishment in his native medium; they simply thought him capable of orthodox greatness in the classical tradition.

Mrs. Fairbanks, of course, urged Mark onward and upward continually. She wrote him about 1880:

> Now, I want you to write another book, in an entirely differ-
> ent style—I can see just what you could do, with some man-
> uscript that you have, and more that you might make, that
> would give you the fresh enjoyment of *surprising* the public.
> Won't you do [it] right away? The time has come for your *best
> book.* I do not mean your most taking book, with the most
> money in it, I mean your best contribution to American liter-
> ature. I have thought of it a great deal of late and wished the
> thought & wish would inspire you my boy.

Edwin Pond Parker, the preacher who made a hobby of literature, spoke for Mark's well-wishers at home.

> Your rank as a writer of humorous things is high enough—
> but, do you know—Clemens—that it is in you to do some
> first-class serious or sober work.

> Now let me say *to* you what I have repeatedly said *of* you—
> that I know no American writer of your generation, who is
> capable of writing such forcible, sinewy, racy English as you.
> You are abundantly capable of turning out some work that
> shall bear the stamp of your individuality plainly enough,
> and at the same time have a sober character and a solid worth
> & a permanent value. It might not pay in "shekels," but it
> would do you vast honor, and give your friends vast pleasure.

This letter was delivered to Mark at a time when he was
completing a new novel.

In the summer of 1877, Mark began to think seriously
about a book to satisfy his wife, his neighbors, and the
friends elsewhere who hoped to elevate his literary aspirations. Mrs. Theodore Crane, Livy's sister, had in the library
at Quarry Farm a copy of Charlotte M. Yonge's *The Prince
and the Page.* It focused Mark's attention upon Edward VI.
He had been reading English history extensively. During the
winter in Hartford, he recorded in fifty words the central
theme of *The Prince and the Pauper.* Around the accidental
interchange of Edward VI and a guttersnipe he began carefully to construct a picture of sixteenth-century England,
drawing heavily on a half-dozen sources. In February 1878
Mark wrote Mrs. Fairbanks that he was writing a historical
tale of three hundred years ago

> simply for the love of it—for it will appear without my name—
> such grave stately work being considered by the world to be
> above my proper level. I have been studying for it, off & on,
> for a year & a half. I swear the Young Girls' Club to secresy &
> read the MS to them, half a dozen chapters at a time, at their
> meetings. They profess to be very much fascinated with it; so
> do Livy & Susie Warner [wife of local author Charles Dudley
> Warner].

THE PRINCE AND THE PAUPER AS A COMMUNAL EFFORT

Mark was writing rapidly at this time. Since the tale was ostensibly for children, he read the chapters to his daughters and to the girls of the Saturday Morning Club. At one family audience, Susie and Clara perched on the arms of his chair, while Livy listened from across the fire and Mrs. Fairbanks beamed in the background. The adults glowed in the book's "loveliness"; the children were entranced. But by summer, composition had halted in the face of plot difficulties. A long trip to Europe and its record (*A Tramp Abroad*) were completed before he picked up the manuscript again in the fall of 1880. This time he finished the book and began to circulate the manuscript among friends who had not heard him read it aloud. *The Prince and the Pauper* was in a way more theirs than his; he was anxious not to publish it without corroboration from those who had urged him to write it. On Christmas Eve, then, of 1880, he could answer Parker's letter:

> I thank you most sincerely for those pleasant words. They come most opportunely, too, at a time when I was wavering between launching a book of the sort you mention, with my name to it, and smuggling it into publicity with my name suppressed. Well, I'll put my name to it, and let it help me or hurt me as the fates shall direct.

> It is not a large book, so I have not scrupled to ask Howells and Twichell [local pastor and Twain's closest friend] to run over the manuscript and advise me what to modify and what to knock out. I must go warily seeing this is such a wide departure from my accustomed line.

> Howells has read it and he winds up his four pages (mainly of vigorous approval) with the remark—"I think the book will be a great success unless some marauding ass who does not snuff his wonted pasturage there should prevail on all the other asses to turn up their noses in pure ignorance. It is such a book as I would expect from you, knowing what a bottom of substance there is to your fun, but the public at large ought to be led to expect it, and must be."

> Howells found fault with two things, some descriptions of English court ceremonials which he wants shortened, and a story of a boy, a bull, and some bees, which he won't have in the book at all, because he says it lowers its dignity, so I guess I'll have to scratch that out.

> But what I'm coming to is this:—Will you, too, take the manuscript and read it, either to yourself, or, still better, aloud to your family? Twichell has promised me a similar service. I hoped to get criticisms from Howells's children but evidently

he spared them, which was carrying charity too far!

Merry Christmas!
Yours truly,
S.L. Clemens

With Parker, Twichell, Susie and [Dudley Warner's daughter] Lilly Warner, the Saturday Morning Club, and the neighborhood children participating in the criticism of *The Prince and the Pauper*, it became, more than any other book of Mark's, the product of community collaboration. In concession to his friends, he made many changes, excised the extended burlesque of the whipping boy's story, but insisted on retaining some of the phrases his critics objected to, re-

MARK TWAIN ON THE GENTEEL INFLUENCE

In Mark Twain in Eruption, *Bernard DeVoto compiled a number of previously unpublished personal papers written by Mark Twain. In the following excerpt, Twain writes about his experience with airing his views with his Hartford circle and says that while he felt free to talk about his contentious philosophical positions with his neighbors, he was reluctant to publish them.*

[I] have never much minded whether my listeners liked [what I had to say] or not, but I couldn't get beyond that—the idea of actually publishing always brought me a shudder; by anticipation I couldn't bear the reproaches which would assail me from a public which had been trained from the cradle along opposite lines of thought and for that reason—which is a quite sufficient reason—would not be able to understand me.

I had early proved all this, for I laid one chapter of my gospel [from *What Is Man?* published after Twain's death] before the Monday Evening Club in Hartford, a quarter of a century ago, and there was not a man there who didn't scoff at it, jeer at it, revile it, and call it a lie, a thousand times a lie! That was the chapter denying that there is any such thing as personal merit; maintaining that a man is merely a machine automatically functioning without any of his help or any occasion or necessity for his help, and that no machine is entitled to praise for any of its acts of a virtuous sort nor blamable for any of its acts of the opposite sort. Incidentally, I observed that the human machine gets all its inspirations from the outside and is not capable of originating an idea of any kind in its own head; and I further remarked, incidentally, that no man ever does a duty for duty's sake but only for the sake of the satisfac-

ry.

fusing in particular to strike out one "blot" Twichell and Parker caviled at. The book was gradually made ready for the press during 1881 while the community waited eagerly to learn the reaction of the critics and of the public.

A LONE VOICE

Only one uneasy voice was raised to question the fitness of Mark Twain's dabbling in romance. Joseph T. Goodman, the editor who had recognized Mark's gifts in Nevada and helped him map out his literary territory, learned what was going on in Hartford. He wrote in October, 1881:

I see mention of your forthcoming, "Prince and Pauper," stat-

tion he personally gets out of doing the duty, or for the sake of avoiding the personal discomfort he would have to endure if he shirked that duty; also I indicated that there is no such thing as free will and no such thing as self-sacrifice.

The club handled me without gloves. They said I was trying to strip man of his dignity, and I said I shouldn't succeed, for it would not be possible to strip him of a quality which he did not possess. They said that if this insane doctrine of mine were accepted by the world life would no longer be worth living, but I said that that would merely leave life in the condition it was before.

Those were the brightest minds in Hartford—and indeed they were very superior minds—but my little batch of quite simple and unassailable truths could get no entrance into them, because the entrances were all stopped up with stupid misteachings handed down by stupid ancestors and docilely accepted without examination, whereas until those minds should be unstopped they would not be competent to intelligently examine my gospel and intelligently pass upon it. No mind, howsoever brilliant, is in a condition to examine a proposition which is opposed to its teachings and its heredities until, as pointed out by Lord Bacon some centuries ago, those prejudices, predilections, and inheritances shall have been swept away. I realized that night that since those able men were such children, such incompetents, in the presence of an unfamiliar doctrine, there could be but one result if my gospel should be placed before the general public: it would make not a single convert and I should be looked upon as a lunatic, besides; therefore I put aside the idea of elaborating my notions and spreading them abroad in a book.

Mark Twain in Bernard DeVoto's *Mark Twain in Eruption*, 1968, pp. 240–41.

ing that it is a story of remote English life. I'm very impatient to see it, for of all things I have been anxious that you try your hand at another novel. But what could have sent you groping among the driftwood of the Deluge for a topic when you would have been so much more at home in the wash of today?

It was a good question. Goodman anticipated the opinion of posterity by preferring the disorderly representation of contemporary American life in *Roughing It* (written with Goodman's assistance) to the ingenious, pleasant, but superficial *Prince*. He was too far away to interfere effectively with the influences which in this single instance turned Mark from his proper materials to the only consciously "literary" book he wrote during his Hartford residence.

NOVEL AS TWAIN'S MASTERPIECE

Nook Farm was charmed, of course, when the book appeared during the Christmas season of 1881 in the gaudiest format Osgood could contrive. A December 28, 1881, *Courant* editorial written by Warner or Parker welcomed Mark to the company of great and serious writers:

> Mark Twain has finally fulfilled the earnest hope of many of his best friends, in writing a book which has other and higher merits than can possibly belong to the most artistic expression of mere humor.

Of course, the humorist should not be undervalued, the reviewer said; he has a mission higher than provoking the "guffaws of the gaping crowd."

> There is a humorous aspect of human life and of human affairs, the successful presentation of which not only excites mirth but dispels many an illusion, pricks many a bubbled conceit, and exposes many a cheap fallacy and thin sentiment as could be done by no other means so well.

> Nevertheless the functions and office of the humorist in literature are somewhat limited. His honor is not likely to be durable.

With this new book Mark Twain revealed himself a diligent and thoughtful student of English classical literature and strengthened his claim to the most vigorous style of his age. The excellences and charms of the romance

> are such as only a man of genius, writing with a sober if not serious purpose and with utmost literary sincerity, could furnish. The conception of the story is unique and original, the intricate plot is developed with admirable clearness, and the inherent improbability at the base of the story is so artistically treated that one quite forgets it till the end is reached.

A few blemishes of slang and a few inappropriate humorous exaggerations should have been expunged in judicious revision, but the book is nevertheless occasion for congratulations on the attainment of a new honor in literature. "May he soon try again!"

Mark's other friends concurred. Mrs. Fairbanks was rapturous. Her husband wept over the book, except when he came upon some "Munchausen element [an exaggeration or tall tale]." The book, she said, was his "masterpiece in fineness." When would he do another? There was time for another. And since he was fortunate to breathe the inspiring air of Hartford, he would find there occasion for a second masterpiece. Mrs. Stowe, similarly susceptible, was to read the book over and over with childlike delight. In April of 1887, Harriet encountered Mark on the sidewalk, took both his hands, and told him with a fervency which brought tears to his eyes: "I am reading your *Prince and Pauper* for the fourth time, and I *know* it is the best book for young folks ever written." Six weeks later she came upon the Ombra to announce completion of her sixth reading.

Outside Nook Farm, the professional critics whose reviews I have read were unanimous in high praise and pleased by Mark's achievement as a serious writer. They praised his talent for description, plot construction, and character creation, and admired his philosophical inclination and his achievement of a subdued refinement of expression, an ennobling moral, and a pleasant treatment of a far-away epoch. *The Prince and the Pauper* was thought the climax of his craftsmanship.

DISAPPOINTMENT AT REVERSION TO OLD STYLE

At the midpoint of his Hartford residence, then, Mark wrote a book precisely gauged to the taste of Hartford. The delight of his refined friends turned to mild disappointment in the backsliding apparent in his next two works, *Life on the Mississippi* and *Huckleberry Finn*. Eager, in all friendliness, to excuse Mark for abandoning the kind of book it liked most, Hartford sadly attributed his retrogression to the cold reception the salesmen of *The Prince* encountered on all the back roads. Mark's neighbors recognized his professional necessity to please his audience and professed to understand his deference to vulgar taste, but they manufactured and rather enjoyed for a long time the sad irony that America would not let its best writer fully develop his talents. Charles Hopkins Clark [former editor of the *Courant*] spoke at Mark Twain's death in 1910 of Hartford's long-lived regrets:

> If we are not mistaken, the readers of this paragraph will generally agree that his finest book was "The Prince and the Pauper," but it sold the least, and he has been quoted as giving that fact as his reason for not following that line any further.

Speaking somewhat earlier for the critical fraternity at large, [literary critic] Henry Vedder, a sort of weathervane for literary opinion in the nineties, referred to what he considered the ironic likelihood that a humorist can never be taken seriously. Readers failed to enjoy *The Prince and the Pauper* because they looked for a joke and could not find it.

> It is only when, as "Mark Twain," he writes some such trash as "The Adventures of Huckleberry Finn" that this really capable writer can make sure of an appreciative hearing.

The commercial failure of the book was doubtless a strong motive for returning to the Mississippi materials, and it was an excellent reason to furnish to the community. But for all kinds of reasons, Mark could not be completely at home when he was not writing out of his own personal experience. Whatever the motive, Mark abandoned the historical past until he came to complete *A Connecticut Yankee,* chiefly significant in what it says about the present. And in that book the burlesque he had suppressed in *The Prince and the Pauper* ran riot, to disappoint again those who thought it ultimately unworthy of his gifts.

But again, Hartford's disappointment involved no real disapproval of Mark Twain. Supported by a tendency to see a moral seriousness in his humor, his neighbors accepted him as he was. The pressure they exerted was exceedingly mild. Though Parker might long for a tender tale with a moral, Twichell would supply the suggestion for *Old Times on the Mississippi.* And if the community was thrilled by *The Prince* as by no other book, it was enthusiastic about all of Mark's work and felt no active distaste for his relatively rowdy humor. They loved the man. No reservations about the nobility of his literature could diminish their affection for him.

THE NOVEL'S LITERARY ACCOMPLISHMENTS

In connection with the community's recognition of Mark's compulsion to please the taste of the masses, it is significant that the one book he wrote in Hartford in experimental obliviousness to its commercial success and in deference to the genteel tradition is without many of his faults as a writer. Anyone who reads *The Prince and the Pauper* can see in it the most nearly perfect structure of his collected works, the greatest number of consecutive pages unmarred by flagrant burlesque digression, and the clearest realization of consistent tone—a unique achievement in form applied to artificial materials. Restraint, care, and economy accompanied a conscious effort to prove his literary competence outside the area of his professional activity. For the technical excellence, we may credit the amateur and professional critics of Hartford—since he contrived his book with their criticisms in mind—with a partially accurate perception of Mark's faults. The error of people like Edwin Pond Parker was not their insistence on polished technique, but their underestimation of American materials. They preferred charm to realism, the past to the present, the exotic to the homely. The critical intuitions of Nook Farm were not entirely faulty; in no case did they do Mark Twain serious harm. If, in responding to them, Mark had given the same attention to the form of his Mississippi books that he gave to *The Prince and the Pauper,* his great books would have been greater. But he thought of the carefully constructed book as art and of his improvisatory river volumes as business. For art he had little time.

TWAIN'S IMPRINT

Yet even *The Prince and the Pauper* has upon it the signs of Mark Twain's authorship. Just as he refused to delete a reference to Henry VIII's corpse, so he did not altogether yield in other directions. The gentility of his period is refracted, even in this most genteel book, through his own vigor of style and his own individuality. He attempted to have his characters speak in an idiom laboriously constructed out of lists of archaic words and phrases gleaned from his source books. But though he tried seriously to make all the conversation in his costume-piece appropriate, he could not resist a mixture of modern and sixteenth-century idiom. Within the archaic medium, he often managed considerable vigor. The connective passages, monosyllabic and concise, sometimes return to the Mississippi for their imagery. The description of the rogues who torment the prince is built upon the vivid concreteness and particularity of Mark's most characteristic work. But despite unmistakable signs of his authorship, the subordination of his usual manner to conventional treatment of a charming and instructive tale was almost complete. Mark kept himself out of the book; the personages he substituted for his normal cast of characters have little life. He had not met them on the river.

Documenting the Historical Sources

Leon T. Dickinson

In his article on *The Prince and the Pauper* published in 1949, Leon T. Dickinson of the University of
Missouri, writes about how Mark Twain used the
major sources for his novel and, more importantly,
why he took such pains to document the facts he in-
corporated into his story. Dickinson says Twain drew
on historical sources for dialogue, description,
scenes, and details, in order to make the novel as realistic as possible. According to Dickinson, Twain's
concern that the novel appear historically accurate
was primarily to draw attention to the severity of actual British laws and statutes of the day. This authenticity was also linked to Twain's own theory of fiction. In the nineteenth century the novel was a
relatively new form of literature and Twain, like his
peers, still considered fact-based fiction of greater literary merit than works drawn totally from the cast
of the author's mind.

Mark Twain, we usually say, was a remarkably independent
writer, one who wrote primarily from experience and was
anything but bookish. Such a view has, of course, much
truth in it. And yet he did refer to books in his writing. We
know that he read about foreign countries before and during
the writing of the travel books. He read widely, also, in
preparing to write his historical books. Of these, *The Prince
and the Pauper* offers some interesting problems. It is clear
what the sources are, for Clemens acknowledges his indebt-
edness in notes appearing at the end of the volume. I am
concerned with how he used the sources and why he admitted dependence on them.

The work most frequently cited in connection with Clemens'

Reprinted from "The Sources of *The Prince and the Pauper*," by Leon T. Dickinson,
Modern Language Notes, pp. 103–106, February 1949. Copyright © 1949 by The Johns
Hopkins University Press. Reprinted with permission from The Johns Hopkins Uni-
versity Press.

book is Charlotte M. Yonge's juvenile, *The Prince and the Page* (1865). No critic, however, points to similarities in the two books, for they are entirely different. Clemens' biographer believed that the earlier story, an historical romance laid in the thirteenth century, might have "inspired" the later tale; but, he concludes, rightly, that "no comparison of any sort is possible between them."

SOURCES CREATE AUTHENTICITY

He did borrow from books, however, in writing *The Prince and the Pauper*, as can be seen from his appended notes. Some of these refer to the book of his Hartford friend, J. Hammond Trumbull, entitled *The True-Blue Laws of Connecticut and New Haven and the False Blue-Laws*. Trumbull's book was written to show that the laws of seventeenth-century Connecticut were not so foolish or so severe as were commonly supposed, and that compared to the English statutes of the same period, the Connecticut laws were humane and enlightened, a point that Mark Twain makes in a "General Note" at the end of his volume. In order to show that what was harsh in the Connecticut laws was of English origin, Trumbull included in his introduction several cases involving infringement of the severe laws in England during the sixteenth and seventeenth centuries. It was from these cases, as his notes show, that Mark Twain borrowed for his story—borrowed accounts of persons losing their ears, being branded, being burned to death, boiled to death (sometimes in oil), hanged for such offenses as larceny above twelve pence, stealing a horse, a hawk, and so on.

Another source which he used in much the same way was *The English Rogue*, a seventeenth-century English book by Richard Head and Francis Kirkman. Several details in Chapters 17 and 18 of *The Prince and the Pauper* he took, sometimes without acknowledgment, from Chapters 5, 6, and 7 of the English tale. Clemens' chapters treating the low life of London include canting terms, a snatch of song, dialogue, description, and episodes, all of which are to be found in *The English Rogue*. At times he sticks close to his original, as is evident from the following passages, dealing with the set speech of beggars asking for coins:

The English Rogue	*The Prince and the Pauper*
For Gods sake some tender hearted Christians,	" . . . o' God's name cast through your merciful

cast through your merci-   eyes one pitiful look
ful eyes one pittiful look   upon a sick, forsaken,
upon a sore, lame, and   and most miserable
miserable wretch: Be-   wretch; bestow one little
stow one penny or half-   penny out of thy riches
penny upon him that is   upon one smitten of God
ready to perish, &c.   and ready to perish!"

At other times Mark Twain elaborates on his original, as, for instance, when he takes an episode, treated in two pages in the source, and expands it to fill six pages, adding detail and dialogue that make the incident more dramatic. But whether he followed his source closely or whether he elaborated on it, he borrowed for the same purpose: to give an air of authenticity to his book. He read a good deal to prepare himself for writing the book, and he was interested not only in making it authentic, but in making it *appear* authentic.

Several points are clear regarding Clemens' use of sources in *The Prince and the Pauper:* (1) he used source material to acquaint himself with the period he was writing about; (2) for the most part he followed his sources quite closely, taking specific things from them; (3) usually, but not always, he acknowledged his debt to a source, either in a footnote or in a note at the end of the volume. This last point calls for comment.

TWAIN'S SERIOUS PURPOSE

Granted that he had a respect for facts, why did Clemens want to document a work of fiction? Two explanations seem likely. One has to do with his purpose in writing the book. He wrote with serious intent, trying to give his readers "a realizing sense of the exceeding severity of the laws of that day by inflicting some of their penalties upon the King himself and allowing him a chance to see the rest of them applied to others." So anxious was he for the book to be taken seriously, that he considered publishing it anonymously. Regarded at the time strictly as a funny man, he feared that the name Mark Twain on the title page would inevitably suggest humor. If the documentation were missing, certainly some of the details of the story would seem, to one unacquainted with Tudor history, to be Mark Twain "whoppers." It was precisely this that Clemens wanted to avoid.

The other explanation concerns Mark's theory of fiction. Fiction based on fact, he seemed to think, was superior to purely imaginative writing. We are told in *The Gilded Age,* for instance, that "The incidents of the explosion [of a steamboat] are not invented. They happened just as they are told." Similarly, in the preface to *Tom Sawyer,* Clemens writes: "Most of the adventures recorded in this book really occurred." He makes the same point in the preface to *A Connecticut Yankee:* "The ungentle laws and customs touched upon in this tale are historical, and the episodes which are used to illustrate them are also historical." Again, a footnote at the beginning of Chapter 1 in *Tom Sawyer, Detective* is to the same effect: "Strange as the incidents of this story are, they are not inventions, but facts—even to the public confession of the accused." If the story is true, Clemens thought, if it is based on fact, it is somehow better than if it were wholly imaginary. Such a theory of fiction, common enough in the West of his day, would go far toward explaining the presence of documentation in *The Prince and the Pauper.*

The Novel in Its Literary Context

Marcus Cunliffe

The following extract is from an article on Twain's English novels written by Marcus Cunliffe for *The Times Literary Supplement* in 1981. In the article Cunliffe summarizes modern critical reaction to *The Prince and the Pauper* and *A Connecticut Yankee in King Arthur's Court.* He describes the debate as to how close these novels were to Twain's life, his beliefs, and his volatile attitude toward England and the monarchy. Cunliffe asserts, however, that the novels should be judged in terms of the literary context of their day. He claims Twain's initial success was related to the gap which was created by the early deaths of Charles Dickens and W.M. Thackeray, writers with notably similar careers to his own. While Twain's individuality and achievement are not in question, Cunliffe concludes that Twain's English novels were shaped by the literary climate of the times that favored this type of historical fiction.

Samuel L. Clemens (or "see *Mark Twain,*" in the way that indexes and encyclopaedias shunt us to the more famous penname) was born in 1835 and died in 1910. It is generally felt that Twain's best work was done in his forties and fifties, ranging from *The Adventures of Tom Sawyer* (1876) to *The Tragedy of Pudd'nhead Wilson* (1894), with *Life on the Mississippi* (1883) and *Huckleberry Finn* (1884) probably the central summit of his achievement. Sam Clemens quit Hannibal, Missouri, before he was a grown man, and later on went back there only to gather notes for the autobiographical *Life on the Mississippi.* By then he was a well-established resident of New England, living in Hartford, Connecticut, in prosperous proximity to such other celebrities as Harriet

Excerpted from "Mark Twain and His English Novels," by Marcus Cunliffe, *The Times Literary Supplement*, December 25, 1981. Reprinted with permission from *The Times Literary Supplement.*

Beecher Stowe. However, it is also generally assumed that Twain was a profoundly *American* writer, drawing his truest inspiration from the great Mississippi Valley of boyhood and youth—the realm of his remembered, inmost heartland.

If this is so, how are we to deal with what might be called his two "English" novels? *The Prince and the Pauper* was published in December 1881. *A Connecticut Yankee in King Arthur's Court* came out eight years after, at the end of 1889. They thus belong chronologically to Twain's most productive period. Do they belong in more important respects? In any case, are they a closely related pair? Several answers—not necessarily congruent one with another—have been offered by critics and biographers. These can be summarized; then a few more may be added.

NOVELS PERIPHERAL TO TWAIN'S DEEPEST CONCERNS

The first argument is that the further Twain departed from America, in time, space and theme, the less sure was his touch. *The Prince and the Pauper* and *A Connecticut Yankee* were set not merely in England but in the past, one in the mid-sixteenth century and the other in a semi-mythical Arthurian kingdom of around 600 AD. Twain liked to read about the past, whether in the Waverley novels of Sir Walter Scott, the diary of Samuel Pepys or Thomas Carlyle's fulminations in *The French Revolution*. He boned up on English history, looking for local colour and for clues to how people actually spoke. But he was not a historian by instinct. Precise accuracy was unimportant to him. Sometimes he attributed to one era behaviour he knew of in connection with a different period. He defended himself by arguing that if the behaviour (usually brutal) had been a feature of a later, supposedly more civilized time, then it was reasonable to infer that such conduct existed earlier.

Twain scholars are apt to brush aside *The Prince and the Pauper*. They may grant that the novel is tighter in construction and more consistent in tone than much of Twain's fiction, including *A Connecticut Yankee*. Otherwise, they tend to classify it with *The Personal Recollections of Joan of Arc* (1896), Twain's subsequent venture into historical romance, as irrelevant to his deepest concerns. *The Prince and the Pauper* is in this view not "American," or is too obliquely so to carry conviction. We are told that Twain yielded to Hartford neighbours who begged him to put his talents to higher use than mere slapstick. He did indeed endeavour to present a reasonably authentic picture of the England of Henry VIII and Henry's heir, Edward VI, imparting (in the slightly coy claim of the subtitle) moral lessons for "young people of all ages." The publication date fitted in with the Christmas gift season. The "historical" narrative style Twain concocted was almost free from Americanisms. He considered publishing the book anonymously; and a reviewer in the *Atlantic Monthly* in fact remarked that "not even a critical expert" would attribute *The Prince and the Pauper* to Mark Twain "if his name were withheld from the title-page." Twain did do this with *Joan of Arc*, introducing it as a *Harper's* magazine serial with his own authorship concealed—as if to deny an essential identity.

The *Connecticut Yankee* has been far more thoroughly worked over by critics, yet often with the intent to account for the book's uncertainty of touch. The London *Spectator* disparaged the novel on publication in 1889 as "coarse and clumsy." An Edinburgh newspaper said it was "a 'lecture' in dispraise of monarchical institutions and religious establishments, and in praise of Yankee cuteness and Wall Street chicanery as compared to the simple fidelity . . . of the knightly ideal." Though such dismissals have been commoner in Britain than in the United States, we can trace a recurrent notion that when Twain strayed too far from home, literarily, he lost his way.

BIOGRAPHICAL CONNECTIONS

A second approach is to maintain that while the *Yankee* is a considerably more interesting work, both novels fit perfectly well into the Twain canon. *The Prince and the Pauper* can for example be shown to reveal the author's lifelong fascination with doubles, twins and reversed identities. The accidental exchange of roles between the boy-prince, England's future king, Edward VI, and Tom Canty, a lad from a London slum, anticipates the switching in *Pudd'nhead Wilson* of a light-hued slave baby and a white infant. The reversal of fortunes that exposes Edward, Prince of Wales, to rags, to hunger and to danger, likewise anticipates the plight in *A Connecticut Yankee* of King Arthur, sold into slavery through error when he accompanies Hank Morgan on an incognito tour of his domain. . . .

So *A Connecticut Yankee* can be thought of as a novel about Twain's America rather than about medieval England. That was the interpretation put forward by Twain's close friend the critic-novelist William Dean Howells, reviewing *A Connecticut Yankee* with almost uncritical amity. Twain, "our arch-humorist," in Howells's words, transcended mere humour. "At every moment the scene amuses, but it is all the time an object-lesson in democracy. It makes us glad of our republic and our epoch; but it does not flatter us into a fond content with them"—for, Howells suggested, the noble of King Arthur's day was shown to be basically identical to the exploitative entrepreneur of nineteenth-century Britain or America. . . .

Much of this commentary is concerned with the complexities of Clemens/Twain. Henry Nash Smith and Justin Kaplan have analysed Twain's increasing difficulty in completing any book. *The Prince and the Pauper* was four interrupted years in the making. *A Connecticut Yankee* involved a still more distracted struggle. Twain was preoccupied with the Paige typesetting machine, on which he staked his and his wife's resources in the expectation that the perfected invention would revolutionize printing and bring him a vast fortune. The Paige machine, however, remained intricately imperfect. Its failure bankrupted Twain, forcing him to sell his Hartford home and live abroad in Europe during most of the 1890s. Hence, some biographers surmise that in the gradual turn in *A Connecticut Yankee* from pride in nineteenth-century know-how to the grim finale . . . the dream of glorious modernity goes awry. So did the author's own fantasy of becoming a tycoon—greater than Jay Gould, on a par with the multimillionaire Andrew Carnegie, with whom Twain was delighted to be on first-name terms. . . .

The blend of criticism and biography has been a conspicuous feature of Twain scholarship. Not surprisingly: his writing is, to a degree unusual among authors, personal in tone and at least implicitly autobiographical. Twain's unevenness, his abrupt shifts of plot, the jump from joke to sobriety, and from one level of humour to another, prompt us to seek explanations in the contrarieties of Clemens the man.

TWAIN'S AMBIVALENCE TO GREAT BRITAIN

For instance, it is tempting to see his ambivalent judgments on rulers and ruled, elites and mobs, as signs of an innate dualism. Clemens/Twain was descended on one side of the family from the Lambtons—Earls of Durham who even up to his day professed a strong attachment to visions of me-

dieval chivalry. On the other side he claimed descent from a
regicide judge: a man associated with sending King Charles
I to the scaffold in 1649.

This dualism has been charted by Howard D. Baetzhold
(Mark Twain and John Bull: The British Connection) as an al-
ternating dislike of and admiration for Great Britain, with admiration eventually coming out on top. Twain's final visit to
England, to receive an honorary doctorate from Oxford University, was for him a marvelous accolade; and it brought his
Atlantic crossings to a grand total of thirty-one. The figure is
a reminder that he was an enthusiastic traveller and that he
often turned toward England. He stayed for several months in
1872, and again twice in 1873–74. He toured the Continent in
1878–79, winding up with another English visit.

TWAIN'S IRREVERENCE

*In a biting yet playful response to comments like that of
Matthew Arnold on America and Americans, Twain said:*

One of the most trying defects which I find in these—these—
what shall I call them? for I will not apply injurious epithets
to them, the way they do to us, such violations of courtesy being repugnant to my nature and my dignity. The farthest I can
go in that direction is to call them by names of limited reverence—names merely descriptive, never unkind, never offen-
sive, never tainted by harsh feeling. If *they* would do like this,
they would feel better in their hearts. Very well, then—to proceed. One of the most trying defects which I find in these
Stratfordolaters, these Shakesperiods, these thugs, these ban-
galores, these troglodytes, these herumfrodites, these blather-
skites, these buccaneers, these bandoleers, is their spirit of irreverence. It is detectable in every utterance of theirs when
they are talking about us. I am thankful that in me there is
nothing of that spirit. When a thing is sacred to me it is impossible for me to be irreverent toward it. I cannot call to
mind a single instance where I have ever been irreverent, except toward the things which were sacred to other people.

Mark Twain, *What Is Man?* 1917.

During the 1870s Twain was on the whole an emphatic
anglophile. What he cherished, and what he missed in his
own country, was the honest efficiency of government, local
and national, and the enduring appeal of tradition. During
the 1873 visit he told an American friend, with lyric wistful-

ness, of his emotion in glimpsing Admiral Nelson's Victory—
"that colossal & superb old ship, all beflagged . . . & her old
historical signal flying at her masthead once more. . . . God
knows I wish we had some of England's reverence for the
old & great."

Not long afterward, in 1875, Twain contributed an anony-
mous satire, "The Curious Republic of Gondour," to the *Atlantic Monthly*. The essay amounted to a condemnation of
American-type universal suffrage, and a definite preference
for a society graded through education and traditional
wealth like that of Britain. In his imaginary paradise of Gondour, every citizen had one basic vote. But a person could receive up to nine votes; the additions were reckoned on an
ascending scale of educational attainment plus affluence. In
a letter of 1877 Twain, probably without any tinge of irony,
asserted that "Republican Government, with a sharply restricted suffrage, is just as good as Constitutional monarchy
with a virtuous & powerful aristocracy; but with an unre-
stricted suffrage it ought to . . . perish because it is founded
in wrong & it is weak & bad & tyrannical."

By 1881, when he finished *The Prince and the Pauper*,
Twain's estimate of republican democracy was more favour-
able, at least by the negative gauge of Reformation England.
Edward as prince and monarch, hitherto utterly ignorant of
the miseries of the poor, begins to learn only when thrown
among beggars and thieves. The lesson takes a while to sink
in: "Carve me this rabble to rags!" is his imperious cry on being rescued from a mob. Still, Edward does eventually real-
ize that "kings should go to school to their own laws . . . , and
so learn mercy." All ends happily enough. Tom Canty the
pauper and other worthy persons are properly rewarded for
their loyal services. Though Edward VI died after only a few
years on the throne, Twain concedes that his reign was "singularly merciful for those harsh times." Edward's courage is
never in doubt; nor are his innate intelligence and decency.

ANTI-ENGLAND STANCE IN THE 1880s

Anglophilia, we are told, gave way during the 1880s in Twain
to irritability and then to fury. One stimulus was *The People's
History of the English Aristocracy*, a book sent to Twain in
1887 by its radical English author George Standring. Standring edited a magazine called *The Republican* and insisted
that hereditary privilege was a fatal impediment to the de-

velopment of democracy in Britain. The same argument coloured *Triumphant Democracy* (1886), a hymn of praise to America by the Scottish-born magnate Andrew Carnegie. Twain, thanking Carnegie for the book in 1890, misnamed it "The Triumphant Republic," and claimed it "helped to fire me up" for the writing of *A Connecticut Yankee.*

Twain's pendulum-swing towards anglophobia, if that is what it was, can also be inferred from his touchy response to various pronouncements by Matthew Arnold, who unlike that other distinguished critic, Howells, was not an old friend of Twain's. In various articles and lectures of the 1880s, Arnold decided that the United States was not distinguished, or "interesting." Americans lacked reverence: a deficiency manifest in their "addiction to the 'funny man.'". . .

A CHANGE OF HEART

Scholars offer various theories to account for his renewed politeness towards England [in the 1890s]. How could such an outright republican find himself paying lavish tribute to Queen Victoria—a unique monarch, he said, surpassing the virtuous young Edward VI in her dedication to "lofty ideals"—on the occasion of her Diamond Jubilee in 1897? One argument is that with old age Twain became more radical and more focused, that his new targets—Russia's Tsarist régime, the horrors perpetrated in the Congo by Leopold of the Belgians—made the offences supposedly committed by a Matthew Arnold appear negligible. This thesis can be restated to stress Twain's mounting pessimism—a deterministic bias so bleak that almost all human activities, virtuous or otherwise, shrank into microscopic insignificance. Twain's final, posthumous novel, *The Mysterious Stranger* (1916), is also "historical" in that it is set in medieval Austria. Its message, however, is that human history is neither comic nor tragic, neither progressive nor reactionary, but fundamentally unreal.

Pieces of evidence can be produced in support of all the above propositions. There is no doubt, for instance, that as he grew older Mark Twain wavered in his ideas as to the role of humour. Was "fun" mainly a method of amusing, and so winning a mass audience? He obviously cared a great deal about the techniques of comedy, spoken and written: the deadpan delivery, the seeming *non sequitur*, the exact timing of the "clincher." On the other hand, he sought to justify himself, oxymoronically, as a serious entertainer, maintaining that his brand of humour, at least, was inherently humanitarian and reformist. Howells put the point by remarking that except for political humorists, notably J.R. Lowell, American funny men before Twain "chose the wrong side . . . ; they were on the side of slavery, of drunkenness, and of irreligion; the friends of civilization were their prey; their spirit was thoroughly vulgar and base."

Twain commentators have contended that Twain's temperament, and his circle of friends, imposed impossible strains. Certainly we cannot help noticing his lapses into sentimentality, especially in writing about women and children. There is also Twain the entrepreneur—an aspect that led him to attribute to the superintendent-mechanic Hank Morgan talents and ambitions (eg, running a stock exchange) more appropriate to the banking magnate J.P. Morgan. This was the Twain who from time to time announced his imminent retirement from the drudgery of authorship, on the calculation that he could live off royalties and investments.

TWAIN FILLS THE GAP

However valid these explanations, more remains to be said, with emphasis laid on the cultural context rather than Twain's own idiosyncratic biography. Howells was correct in believing that Twain signaled the arrival of some new force in literature which had to do with mood, style, versatility in genre and breadth of appeal. One of the puzzles in Twain's story is how by the early 1870s he was able to gain recognition, at home and in Europe, as an important man of letters. At that stage Twain's *curriculum vitae* included little more than the "Celebrated Jumping Frog" story, popularity as a platform humorist, and *The Innocents Abroad* (1869). The record itself is not big enough to account for his astonishing reception in the Anglo-American literary realm. The popularity came, I think, because he filled a gap—the need hitherto met by W.M. Thackeray and Charles Dickens, who died in 1863 and 1870 respectively. Thackeray and Dickens both began as humorists (with comic pseudonyms), yet evolved into more serious art. Both were versatile, and prolific. Both lectured, Dickens with especial histrionic flair. In 1846 both brought out travel narratives, Thackeray the *Notes of a Journey from Cornhill to Grand Cairo* and Dickens the *Pictures from Italy*, which combined solemn art-appreciation with passages of facetious swagger. Both as professional authors produced for the Christmas market. Both tried their hand at historical novels (Thackeray's *Henry Esmond*, Dickens's *A Tale of Two Cities*). And, to repeat, both died in mid-career, leaving a vacuum that no one else seemed quite equipped to fill. By default, in came the American claimant, Samuel Langhorne Clemens, a.k.a. Mark Twain.

The parallels with Twain are intriguing. And he indeed wrote a play and a novel entitled *The American Claimant* (1892), probably inspired by the case of the Tichborne Claimant, the English real-life drama of the early 1870s which Twain had followed with avid interest. The claimant to the Tichborne family fortune was deemed to be a fraud, and so was Colonel Sellers, the American "heir" of Twain's story. At no conscious level, however, did he think that he had stepped into someone else's shoes, or that he was inferior in quality. We do know that Twain said he had never been able to laugh at *Pickwick Papers*, the book that brought early fame to Dickens. Moreover, he came to detest his one-time friend Bret Harte, and counted among Harte's faults a tendency to plagiarize, from Dickens. In 1879, too, he was bruised by a clipping from a London newspaper which preferred Harte's humour as "more English and less thoroughly Yankee" than Twain's, and added that the crude lack of reverence in *Innocents Abroad* would prevent such humour from ever reaching the heights occupied by Dickens and Thackeray.

LITERARY PRESTIGE OF THE HISTORICAL ROMANCE

Consciously or not, Mark Twain did achieve an Anglo-American renown almost as great as that of Sir Walter Scott, more popularly based than that of the gentlemanly Thackeray, and possibly equivalent to that of the spectacularly self-made entertainer-moralist Dickens. Scott was the only one of the three Twain publicly disparaged—and this (from *Life on the Mississippi)* mainly in the guise of an indictment of the false chivalry of the American South, which he blamed on an excessive appetite for reading Scott's romances. Twain studied Scott, however, in preparation for his own ventures into historical fiction; and there is clear evidence that he felt such an endeavour was fitting for important authors on the plane he had attained with Thackeray, Dickens and perhaps that other prolific, well-known British novelist, Bulwer Lytton.

In other words, Twain regarded historical fiction as a genuine challenge. It sold well, in Britain and in America. Authors as famous as Dickens and Twain must win approval on both sides of the Atlantic; hence the passionate interest of both men to improve international copyright protection. Some of this work was designed for the increasingly sizeable juvenile market. Twain himself admitted that he had picked up notions for *The Prince and the Pauper* from Charlotte M. Yonge, whose tales of English history for young people included *The Little Duke* and *The Prince and the Page.* He convinced himself that his own book had stimulated Frances Hodgson Burnett to write her best-selling *Little Lord Fauntleroy* (1886). Twain's *Prince and the Pauper* was intended to sell, to readers of all ages and as many countries as possible (not surprisingly, he was eager to be published in other languages). But on some higher plane, *The Prince,* like *Joan of Arc* and (more confusedly) *A Connecticut Yankee,* was visualized by Twain not as a hasty commercial offering, but as a demonstration of his full literary armament.

Despite mock-humorous disclaimers, Twain felt he could speak to a worldwide audience, as Dickens had done. In part this was because of the universality of humour. In part it derived from his own unvarying certainty: that the best English was now being written by Americans, and that the *very* best came from his pen. We should add that, hostile reviewers aside, a multitude of people agreed with him. . . .

To be made an Oxford D Litt, in 1907, was almost to suggest that the republic of letters was better understood as a kingdom. "King" was in fact the nickname given to Twain by his court of intimates in these last years.

This is not to say he was ultimately an anglophile. On the contrary: he resented the overlordship of English literature, and exulted in the belief that the Americans had taken "the bulk of the shares" in the "joint stock company" of their common language, with himself the chief speculator in cornering the market. He felt the process was an Americanizing one, but also that slang or hyperbole were by no means the only American modes. Pure diction and universal/historical material were available to every master of the British or American culture.

THE LITERARY CLIMATE AND CULTURE

In the process, Twain was a prominent figure, but only one of several; and like them he was influenced by more than purely personal concerns. In a literary sense it is doubtful

whether any author directly "influenced" him. He was entitled to take pride in his wayward originality. Nevertheless, a
quite considerable quantity of novels and stories in the Anglo-American literary domain are close enough to his to
show that certain problems, plots and so on were in the
common air. Some of these are often mentioned; for instance, the dual personality theme in Robert Louis Stevenson's *Dr Jekyll and Mr Hyde* (1886). Another much-read
novel, Rider Haggard's *King Solomon's Mines* (1885) anticipates Hank Morgan: Haggard's hero, in peril among savages,
overawes them through foreknowledge that a solar eclipse is
about to occur. The exchange of roles in *The Prince and the
Pauper* can be compared to F. Anstey's comic English novel
Vice Versa (1882), in which a wretched schoolboy is delighted to change places with his father Mr Bultitude, a
pompous business man. In 1889, the same year as *A Connecticut Yankee,* another American humorist, the whimsical
Frank Stockton, published *The Great War Syndicate,* an ingenious fantasy of future technological combat. . . .

It is important to grasp that in the last third of the nineteenth century dozens of authors, British and American and
some from other countries, drew eclectically upon a large
available stock of genres and motifs. Some, including R.L.
Stevenson and Rudyard Kipling, went beyond Twain in at
least one respect: they were fluent versifiers where he had to
content himself with notebook doggerel. Some, such as Stockton and Jerome K. Jerome, never quite broke out of the limit-
ing conventions of middlebrow entertainment. Some engaged
themselves in the relatively new field of detective fiction. Several—Jules Verne, Edward Bellamy, H.G. Wells—addressed
themselves to what has become known as "futurology."

Several others looked back, often to Tudor or Plantagenet
England. A few hinted at burlesque, perhaps remembering the
absurd fiasco of the Eglinto Tournament of 1839—a romantic
pageant in Scotland washed out by rain. Most though were
more or less in earnest. The American Charles Major, for example, sold many thousands of copies of his historical romance *When Knighthood Was in Flower* (1898). It and similar
novels prompted Howells to complain that of current literature "nothing of late has been heard but the din of arms, the
horrid tumult of the swashbuckler swashing on his buckler."

The more ambitious a writer, the more diversely experimental as a rule, and perhaps the more restless. Bulwer Lytton

had a go at almost everything, even a novel of the future *(The Coming Race)*. Arthur Conan Doyle, unhappy at being confined to the exploits of Sherlock Holmes, ventured both into historical fiction and into stories of ultra-modern combat.

SUPERIOR WRITER IN THE GENRE

Mark Twain was shaped by this Anglo-American milieu. He also helped to shape it, being more gifted and no more erratic than a number of his contemporaries. As an American, he had indeed started out as a "funny man," he was perhaps under exceptional pressure to prove himself entitled to equal Thackeray and Dickens. We may still feel that his very best work was located in the Mississippi Valley. But he *was* versatile. He wished to prove himself so. He did genuinely share the complex enthusiasm of his age for historical romance. He had, he told Howells, felt "jubilant" in the writing of *The Prince and the Pauper*—at ease, confident in his power to bring the past alive in the present. Mark Twain's forays into English and European history were in his own estimates as justified as, perhaps finer than, all his other writings. If we do not altogether share this view, it merits sympathetic consideration. And, whatever our reservations as to Twain's skill at historical pastiche, a glance at the efforts of other authors in the same vein helps to bring out his decisive superiority.

Nineteenth-Century Critical Reaction

Arthur Lawrence Vogelback

Arthur Lawrence Vogelback, professor of American
Literature at Mary Washington College, has written
extensively on Mark Twain and in particular on critical reaction to Twain's major novels. In the following article, he analyzes the qualities of *The Prince
and the Pauper* which so impressed the critics of the
time. These included the novel's style, artistry, character portrayal, and plot construction. *The Prince and
the Pauper* was, in their view, the first book which
showed a philosophical or serious side to the humorist. Vogelback accounts for the novel's popularity
by showing that it was entirely consistent with the
gentle, refined, and subdued narratives of the day.
The more gritty and realistic style of works like *Tom
Sawyer* and *The Adventures of Huckleberry Finn* per-
turbed nineteenth-century critics, and they therefore
tended to denigrate these novels.

With the appearance in 1869 of *Innocents Abroad,* Mark Twain
established himself as a "funny man," and it was as the work
of a funny man that each new book of his was interpreted.
While there were occasional comments along the way which
revealed a growing appreciation of abilities in Clemens other
than that of mere humorist, for the most part there appeared
little disposition by critics to take him seriously. But with the
publication of *The Prince and the Pauper* in 1881, there sprang
up sudden and widespread recognition of unusual qualities in
Clemens the writer, qualities which caused many reviewers to
express astonishment that such a work could have been written by Mark Twain. Remarked the Boston *Transcript:* "There
is little in the book to remind one . . . of the author," and the
Atlantic Monthly significantly titled its review: "Mark Twain's
New Departure." [Literary critic William Dean] Howells sum-

Reprinted from "*The Prince and the Pauper:* A Study in Critical Standards," by Arthur
Lawrence Vogelback, *American Literature,* March 1942. Copyright © 1942 by Duke
University Press. Reprinted with permission from Duke University Press.

marized this attitude when, after dealing with the fictional elements in Clemens's story, he stated: ". . . we have indicated its
power in this direction rather than in its humorous side, because this has struck us as peculiarly interesting in the work
of a man who has hitherto been known only as a humorist—
a mere farceur—to most people."

It will be profitable as a study in the critical standards of
the day to inquire what were these "new" qualities in *The
Prince and the Pauper* which so pleased the critics, and why
the critics liked them. This will be best shown by a consideration of the critical reaction to Mark Twain, not only as fic-
tionist—that is, as writer of description, stylist, architect of
plot, and depicter of character—but also as "philosopher."

TWAIN'S POWERFUL DESCRIPTION

Previous to the publication of *The Prince and the Pauper*,
there had been little recognition of Mark's talents as a descriptive writer. Occasionally there occurred an appreciative
comment, but for the most part attention remained incidental. When some clearer-visioned critic like Howells insisted
upon unusual descriptive talents in Twain, his voice rarely
found echoes in other reviews. But with the publication of
The Prince and the Pauper, the majority of critics awoke to a
sharp realization of Twain's powerful descriptive gifts. This
was reflected not only in the increased attention given in reviews to the descriptive portions of the book, but in the importance accorded those portions. Thus the *Transcript* took
note of Twain's "vivid descriptive powers," and another
critic, praising "the skillfully painted background of more
subdued and often delicate description," belatedly called the
attention of the reader to "the many picturesque passages in
'Innocents Abroad' and 'A Tramp Abroad.'" At the same time
the accuracy of Clemens's description was commented on.
Said the *Critic:* "It is obvious that Mark Twain has taken considerable pains in bringing the local color of his story into
harmony with the historic period in which the action is
laid," and the reviewer in the *Transcript* acknowledged that
"the local coloring of the time in which [the story] is laid—
that of Edward VI—is carefully studied," a judgment that
was echoed by *Harper's*, which found in the story "a careful
regard for the historical accessories." One of the most flat-
tering observations on this aspect of Clemens's writing came
from the *Atlantic Monthly:*

However skillful in invention a writer may be, it is certain that his work loses nothing of effect from a studious harmonization with the period in which it is placed. In *The Prince and the Pauper* this requirement has been scrupulously observed. The details are never made obtrusive, and the "local color" is never laid on with excess; but the spirit of the age preceding that of Elizabeth is maintained with just the proper degree of art to avoid artfulness. Critical examination shows that no inconsiderable labor has been given to the preservation of this air of authenticity. . . . It is in every way satisfactory to observe that the material accessories are brought into view with an accuracy that coherently supports the veracity of the narrative. Dresses, scenery, architecture, manners and customs suffer no deviation from historical propriety.

NEW STYLE MERITS PRAISE

It is notable, too, that *The Prince and the Pauper* was the first work of Clemens's in which his ability as a stylist received attention. Most of the reviewers registered not a little surprise at the difference between the former style of Clemens and that exhibited in the new book. The *Transcript,* for example, remarked: "There is little in the book to remind one of the individual style of the author," and the *Atlantic Monthly* commented similarly:

> There is nothing in . . . its style of treatment that corresponds with any of the numerous works by the same hand. It is no doubt possible to find certain terms of phraseology, here and there, which belong to Mark Twain . . . but these are few. . . .

Many were the complimentary things said about this aspect of Twain's writing. The *New York Herald* praised the "plastic and finished" style of the book; another journal wrote that "all the charm is owing to the sincerity, the delicacy, and the true feeling with which the story is told . . ."; and the *Transcript,* seeking to describe the style, used the adjectives "vivid" and "natural."

NOTABLE PLOT CONSTRUCTION

Again, *The Prince and the Pauper* was the one book on which most critics were agreed that Twain demonstrated outstanding powers as a constructor of plot. There were, of course, dissenting reviewers. The *Transcript,* for example, remarked that "the highly improbable plot will . . . task the credulity of the most imaginative reader," but the larger number praised Clemens's achievement. To Howells, *The Prince and the Pauper* was definite confirmation of Clemens's ability as plot architect. He prophesied that the book would come in this respect as a surprise to many:

> Like all other romances, it asks that the reader shall take its possibility for granted, but this once granted, its events follow each other not only with probability but with realistic force. The fascination of the narrative . . . [is] felt at once, and increase[s] . . . to the end in a degree which will surprise those who have found nothing but drollery in Mark Twain's books, and have not perceived his artistic sense. . . .

The critic for the *Atlantic Monthly* was inspired by the construction of the tale to point out how remarkably Mark had developed in stature as a writer:

> It will be interesting to watch for the popular estimate of this fascinating book. . . . It has qualities of excellence which [the author] has so long held in reserve that their revelation now will naturally cause surprise. Undoubtedly the plan upon which most of his works have been framed called for neither symmetry, nor synthetic development, nor any of the finer devices of composition. Generally speaking, they serve their purpose without the least reference to the manner in which they were thrown together. . . . Notwithstanding [their merits], they remain the most heterogeneous accumulation of ill-assorted material that ever defied the laws of literature, and kept the country contentedly captive for half a score of years. Now the same public is called upon to welcome its old favorite in a new guise—as author of a tale ingenious in conception . . . artistic in method, and, with barely a flaw, refined in execution.

The *Century Magazine* praised the structure as "an ingeniously formed chain of circumstances," and the *Critic* pointed out that Clemens deserved commendation for the development of a plot which must have "at every step impressed the author as a fertile theme for extravaganza."

REALISTIC CHARACTERS

In the same fashion, with the publication of *The Prince and the Pauper* Clemens came newly, as it were, to the attention of critics as a gifted depicter of character. The reviewer in the *Atlantic Monthly* warmly praised Clemens for the latter's achievement in this regard. After describing the two little boys in the story as "one, a bright figure in history, the other a gem of fiction," the critic made these appreciative comments in which he compared Twain's work with that of a pair of famous English novelists:

> The characters come and go, live and breathe, suffer and rejoice, in an atmosphere of perfect reality, and with a vivid

identity rarely to be found in fictions set in medieval days. The same life-like verisimilitude that is manifest in many pages of Scott, and throughout Reade's *Cloister and the Hearth,* glows in every chapter of this briefer chronicle of a real prince's fancied griefs and perils. To preserve an illusion so consistently, it would seem that the author's own faith in the beings of his creation must have been firm, from beginning to end of their recorded career. . . . The bighearted protector of guileless childhood is as palpable to our senses as to the grateful touch of the prince's accolade. The one soft spot in the hard old monarch's nature reveals itself to our apprehension as clearly as to the privileged courtiers at Westminster. The burly ruffian of the gutters, the patient, sore-afflicted mother, the gracious damsels of pure estate and breeding, the motley vagabonds of the highway, the crafty and disciplined councilors of the realm, the mad ascetic, and the varied throng of participants in the busy scenes portrayed—all these take to themselves the shape and substance of genuine humanity, and stamp themselves to our perceptions as creatures too vital and real to be credited to fable land.

Howells, in his review, likewise pointed out the unusual merits of the character portrayal:

The author has respected his material . . . and has made us feel its finer charm in the delicacy and subtlety with which he has indicated Tom Canty's lapse from lively rebellion at his false position to appreciation of its comforts and splendors, and, finally, to a sort of corrupt resignation in which he is almost willing to deny his poor old mother, when she recognizes him in one of his public progresses. . . . The character of Miles Hendon is dashed in with a rich and bold humor that gives its color to all the incidents of their association. . . . The whimsical devotion with which he humors the boy's royal exactions is charmingly studied . . . amidst the multitude of types with which the story deals, he is realized the best; he is first of all thoroughly recognizable as a man; and then as a man of his own time and country—the adventurous and generous Englishman of the continent-hunting age. . . . The effect of prosperity on the mock Prince is, perhaps, more subtly studied than that of adversity on the real Prince . . . but . . . it is this [latter] phase, apparently . . . which the author most wishes [the reader] to remember. . . .

Perhaps no higher commendation was possible than the remark of the *New York Herald:* "The character of [the] two boys, twins in spirit, will rank with the purest and loveliest creations of child-life in the realm of fiction."

TWAIN AS PHILOSOPHER

Finally, not only were reviewers enthusiastic about *The Prince and the Pauper* as Clemens's first artistic work, but they found in the book even more unusual revelations. They discovered that it demonstrated a philosophical side to Twain. The author had proved himself quite capable of dealing with a profound and serious theme. In almost every review one detects the note of surprise over this aspect of the book. The *Transcript* found "a quality so refined and so searching as to excite wonder that it should flow from the same pen as that which wrote *'The Innocents Abroad'.* . . ." *Harper's* spoke of the tale as being "charged with a generous and ennobling moral." The critic in the *Atlantic Monthly* found the story "pure and humane in purpose"; and the *Century* called the writer of *The Prince and the Pauper* "a satirist and . . . true philosopher." Howells, likewise, found *The Prince and the Pauper* evidence of growth in Clemens:

> The strength of the implied moral [is] felt at once and increase[s] . . . to the end in a degree which will surprise those who have found nothing but drollery in Mark Twain's books, and have not perceived . . . the strain of deep earnestness underlying his humor. Those even who have read him with this perception will recognize an intensified purpose in the human sympathies which have hitherto expressed themselves in some ironical form. The book is in this way an interesting evidence of growth in a man who ought to have his best work before him. The calm of a profound ideal . . . make[s] this a very remarkable book.

And the reviewer in the *Critic* decided with satisfaction that the "finer element" in Mark Twain's nature had at last "hid[den] . . . the humorous vein out of sight."

Novel Complies with Literary Conventions

It appears that the first work on which critics generally agreed that Mark Twain displayed notable abilities as a serious writer and literary artist was *The Prince and the Pauper.* They found the book a praiseworthy departure from his former writing, and they regarded its publication as heralding the advent of a new Clemens. It is time now to ask why this book created such a stir. What were these "new" qualities that so appealed to the critics? Why was it that they ignored a work like *Tom Sawyer* (1876), and poured critical abuse upon the head of Twain when, three years after *The Prince and the Pauper,* his *Huckleberry Finn* (generally acknowledged now as Clemens's finest book) appeared? The answer to these questions may be found in the prevailing critical standards of the day. Reviewers liked the description in *The*

Prince and the Pauper because it was "delicate" and "'subdued." Even the structure was praised on the ground of being
"refined in execution." The characters, too, in *The Prince and
the Pauper* were sweeter and more gentle than such rough-
and-tumble fellows as Tom Sawyer and Huck Finn. The book
dealt pleasantly with a faraway place and epoch, not with the
rude, exuberant frontierland of their own times. The story
was charged with a "pure" and "ennobling" moral; it might
be introduced to any classroom or household without fear of
its consequences to the gentle reader, an advantage which
could not be held out for either *Tom Sawyer* or *Huckleberry
Finn.* In short, critics approved of *The Prince and the Pauper*
because, more than any other of Mark Twain's books up to
that time, it complied with conventional literary ideals.
Works like *Tom Sawyer* or *Huckleberry Finn* puzzled and disturbed the critics; therefore they ignored or denounced them.
But *The Prince and the Pauper* was a work reviewers could
understand; it fitted in perfectly with the tradition of correctness and imitation—with the genteel tradition; and therefore
the critics acclaimed as "new" those qualities in *The Prince
and the Pauper* which were actually least original.

CHAPTER 2

The Novel in Relation to Twain's Other Works

The Prince and the Pauper and Tom Sawyer

Sherwood Cummings

In *Mark Twain and Science: Adventures of a Mind* (1988), Sherwood Cummings, professor of American Literature at California State University in Fullerton, says Twain looked to science for answers to philosophical, social, and moral questions. He was particularly influenced by Hippolyte Taine, a nineteenth-century French philosopher who applied scientific principles to the arts. According to Cummings, Taine had a major influence on the course of American literature which shifted from presenting the world in terms of mythic characters or a Divine plan to "science-based realism" that emphasized the influence of heredity and environment in shaping the human character. Writers began recording the external environments of their central characters in great detail along with their speech, movements, and thoughts. Cummings says *The Prince and the Pauper* was Twain's first modern novel using these principles, and in the following extract contrasts the work with *Tom Sawyer*, an old-fashioned book written before Taine's influence took hold.

The Prince and the Pauper [Mark Twain's first modern novel] reflects both the techniques and the tenets of science-based realism—both the care for detailing significant aspects of environment and the recognition that people are formed by their environments.

CONTEXT AND BACKGROUND

To illustrate Mark Twain's modernization in *The Prince and the Pauper,* we might compare that novel with his previous one, *The Adventures of Tom Sawyer,* an old-fashioned book.

In *Tom Sawyer* there is no program for describing the visible aspects of "the poor little shabby village of St. Petersburg" and its culture. What details are vouchsafed—a sidewalk here, a gate there—are rare and incidental. But in *The Prince and the Pauper* our Tainean historical novelist knows he has to furnish the reader's imagination with the appearance of his chosen time and place. He calls the reader's attention to the plaster, beams, panes, and door hinges of houses; to the gilded gates and granite lions guarding Westminster Palace; to the flat black caps, clerical bands, and blue gowns of the Christ's Hospital boys; to the gilt nails that fasten the crimson velvet to the gold-tasseled halberd staves; to the crutches of the crippled, the eye-patches and string-tied dogs of the blind, and the cant words of the ruffians; to the pail, cup, pots, basin, bench, and stool in the hermit's earth-floor hut; to the hedges, gardens, and sculptured columns of a nobleman's estate; and, pervasively, to the resplendent robes of the nobility and the rags of the poor.

Tom Sawyer's author felt free to introduce him *in medias res,* without past or parents. Tom Canty's author, knowing that a person is the product of past experiences, gave this Tom a detailed case history in a chapter called "Tom's Early Life." There he explained how Tom, though raised in a wretched tenement by a drunken father and an ignorant mother, was secretly educated by a good priest, read books about the lives of princes, pretended that he himself was a prince, and organized his playmates into a royal court. Only with such training could he later be credibly mistaken for a real prince.

TOM CANTY'S AND EDWARD'S CHARACTERS DEVELOP

When it comes to the psychological transformations that Tom Canty and Prince Edward undergo in their switched environments, there is nothing to compare them to in *Tom Sawyer.* They are exceedingly well done, and their mirror-image symmetry is pointed up by elegant touches: Both boys are thought to have gone mad from too much reading and study; both boys on their first night after the switch dream of their former familiar conditions and awaken with dismay to their new, strange surroundings; each boy is given some comfort by a sympathetic "sister"; Tom's first royal meal is touchingly parodied in Edward's first meal in Miles Hendon's quarters; and the courtier's elaborate respect for Tom is mocked by the vagabonds' derision for Edward when they enthrone him as "Foo-foo the First."

Tom's adaptation to the duties and privileges of royalty is understandably easier than Edward's to the insults and deprivations of pauperdom. Tom's first request of his "father," Henry VIII, is to be returned to "the kennel where I was born and bred to misery" and to leave "these pomps and splendors whereunto I am not used." But like Huck Finn before him, who got so he could stand going to school and living in a house, Tom begins to adjust to, even enjoy, his situation. Later that day, when he manages to phrase a courtly sentence, he congratulates himself for having learned from books "some slight trick of their broidered and gracious speech withal." By the third day of his kingship, "he was getting a little used to his circumstances and surroundings; . . . the presence and homage of the great afflicted and embarrassed him less and less sharply with every hour that drifted over his head"; and on the fourth day, "the poor little ash-cat was already more wonted to his strange garret . . . than a mature person could have become in a full month." By the time of his coronation procession, "his heart swelled with exultation" at the sight of worshipful crowds "and he felt that the one thing worth living for in this world was to be a king, and a nation's idol." He becomes so intoxicated with pride that he denies his own mother, who unexpectedly steps out of the crowd to accost him. Immediately thereafter, he is eaten with remorse and his "grandeurs were stricken valueless"; he regains his humility, seeks out his mother, and is rewarded by the true king.

Edward's adjustment to poverty and insolence is much harder but, finally, more spiritually ennobling. Unlike Tom, who comes to deny his own past, Edward never forgets that he is the prince and, on the death of his father, the king of England. "My person is sacred," he screams at the guard who has thrown him, dressed in Tom's rags, out of the palace grounds, "and thou shalt hang for laying thy hand upon me!" He later resolves to hang the jeering boys of Christ's Hospital and to have Tom, his usurper, hanged, drawn, and quartered for treason when he is restored to his throne. He will not allow Miles Hendon to sit in his presence until he has knighted Miles; and when, as an apparent tramp, he does let a charitable peasant woman, who has fed him, sit at her own table, he prides himself on his "gracious humility." A turning point comes when, after several weeks of preserving his autocratic identity in spite of perils and humiliations, he witnesses with horror the kind of punishment he has impulsively wished on people who have crossed him. "That which I have seen," he says, turning away from the fire in which two women are burning for the crime of being Baptist, "will never go out from my memory"; and he resolves that the laws that have "shamed the English name, shall be swept from the statute books." Restored to his throne, and having learned compassion through suffering, he becomes a merciful monarch.

FLAWS IN *THE PRINCE AND THE PAUPER*

The Prince and the Pauper is more "realistic" in technique and theory than *Tom Sawyer*, but that does not mean that Mark Twain's second novel was better than his first. *Tom Sawyer* is too mythic and subjective to be called realistic, yet many readers are likely to find it realer than *The Prince and the Pauper*. What—in spite of the latter novel's "realism," its elegant structure, and its canny psychology—is the matter with it?

Language for one thing. In his working notes, Mark Twain copied a few dozen words and phrases from *Henry IV*, Part 1, and hundreds from *Ivanhoe, Kenilworth,* and *Quentin Durward*, by way of practicing sixteenth-century English. Perhaps if he had reversed the ratio, there would be more Shakespearean vigor and pith in his characters' language— more vivid speeches like this of Miles Hendon to Tom's father: "If thou do but touch him, thou animated offal, I will spit thee like a goose!" Instead, generally, he vaguely imitated Scott, who was himself shamming, or produced locutions [a style of speech] that smacked melodramatically of the popular stage of his own time, as in another speech of Miles Hendon:

> I have lost thee, my poor little mad master—it is a bitter thought—and I had come to love thee so! No! by book and bell, *not* lost. Not lost, for I will ransack the land till I find thee again. Poor child, yonder is his breakfast—and mine, but I have no hunger now—so, let the rats have it—speed, speed! that is the word!

Unfortunately, the stilted dialogue is too often matched by a fake-quaint narrative style. The archaic idioms and genteel abstractions that Mark Twain somehow felt obliged to use in his storytelling give his images a sepia-toned [colorless] dis-

tance and unreality. How can one feel Edward's pain and outrage under the vicious beating he gets from Tom Canty's father and grandmother when the author says, "Between them
they belabored the boy right soundly"? When Tom as king,
looking out of his throne-room window, feels sorry for three
people harassed by a mob, Mark Twain loftily describes his
emotions this way: "The spirit of compassion took control of
him, to the exclusion of all other considerations"; and antic-
ipating the entrance of the three people, Tom "turned his eyes
upon the door with manifestations of impatient expectancy."
It is hard to believe that the author of "Old Times on the Mississippi" could write such polite jargon.

Another problem of the book is the way Mark Twain mon-
keys with history. Uncritical readers might not mind the
Frenchifying of the court, the inflicting of certain seventeenth-
century laws on sixteenth-century vagabonds, or the burning
of Baptists at the stake before Baptists had come into existence. But it must occur to many readers that the climactic
episode, of high moment and total publicity, could not have
happened. The episode is, of course, the ragged Edward's
bursting into Westminster Abbey when Tom is about to be
crowned and, after many public consternations, doubts, tests,
and proofs, succeeding in his demand that he be crowned instead. For authenticity's sake, Mark Twain could have
arranged a behind-the-scenes restoration.

Then, the inevitability of the novel's ideas and action reduces suspense. Beginning as he did with a clear plot outline, instructed as he was in a historian's technique for re-
covering the past, and delighted as he was with his theory
about the formative power of environment, Mark Twain did
not in the process of filling in his outline have much room
for adventuring.

Finally, the novel is less than convincing because (as he
would in general come to understand) it was about a foreign
land and not his own; it was the product of research rather
than of a lifetime of unconscious absorption. But in the
larger picture the novel is important because it introduces
the theme that continued to preoccupy him in *Huckleberry
Finn, A Connecticut Yankee,* and *Pudd'nhead Wilson*—that of
the power of training.

The Prince and the Pauper and Huckleberry Finn

Walter Blair

Mark Twain wrote *The Prince and the Pauper* during a hiatus in the drawn-out preparation of his acclaimed masterpiece *The Adventures of Huckleberry Finn*. In the following extract from *Mark Twain and Huck Finn*, Walter Blair, emeritus professor of English from the University of Chicago, says *The Prince and the Pauper*, though in many ways a "lavish waste of time and talent," was significant on two counts. An analysis of the work illuminates both the development of Twain's personal philosophy and a more profound understanding of his artistically greater novel, *Huckleberry Finn*. Similar characters, plot lines, and themes are evident. Tom Canty, for example, is an amalgam of Tom Sawyer and Huck Finn, and the journey of Edward and Miles Hendon is the sixteenth-century counterpart to that undertaken by Huck and Jim. Furthermore, the loss of romantic notions when encountering the harsh realities of life is a predominant theme in both novels. The major distinguishing feature was in their conclusions. In *The Prince and the Pauper* Twain suggests injustice can be remedied, while by the time he completed *Huckleberry Finn*, he was firmly convinced humanity was beyond redemption.

On hearing that [*The Prince and the Pauper*] was in preparation, Joe Goodman, who had been Clemens' hardbitten boss out in Nevada on the *Enterprise*, wrote to ask him, in effect, what in hell he thought he was up to. In some ways the book was a lavish waste of time and talent. Nevertheless, this novel, with its prettinesses, its prithee-mayhap-enow dia-

Excerpted from *Mark Twain and Huck Finn*, by Walter Blair. Copyright © 1960 by the Regents of The University of California. Reprinted with permission from The University of California Press.

logue, embodies significant attitudes and ideas of its author at the time it was written. And it was written shortly after *Tom Sawyer* and, in part, contemporaneously with *The Tramp Abroad* and *Huckleberry Finn*. Its repetitions of matter in these books and its forecasting of portions of *Huck* are interesting and important.

LINKS WITH TWAIN'S LIFE

Just as *Tom* and *Huck*, set in mid-America of the 1830's or 1840's, recall Clemens' situation in the 1870's so does this novel set in sixteenth-century England. In chapter XX Tom Canty, distressed to hear that the king's expenses outrun his income, says, "We be going to the dogs, 'tis plain. 'Tis meet and necessary that we take a smaller house and set the servants at large. . . ." This sounds like a paraphrase of a letter from Clemens to [his close confidante Mary] Fairbanks. A bit later Tom Canty is depressed by business and like Clemens longs to get away from it all, preferably in the out-of-door world of Tom Sawyer's childhood:

> The dull work went tediously on. Petitions were read, and proclamations, patents, and all manner of wordy, repetitious, and wearisome papers relating to public business; and at last Tom sighed pathetically and murmured to himself, "In what have I offended, that the good God should take me away from the fields and free air and sunshine, to shut me up here . . . and afflict me so."

Again, chapter XXX describes Tom Canty, his love of splendor and his passion for justice, in words that his creator might well apply to himself. In chapter XVII a sixteenth-century robber pays tribute to the eloquence of a woman whose profanity Clemens would have been proud to have uttered: "Cursing them, said I?—cursing them! Why an' thou shouldst live a thousand years thoud'st never hear so masterful a cursing. Alack, her art died with her. There be base and weakling imitators left, but no true blasphemy." Such rhapsodic praise of eloquent profanity is rarely found even today in children's books.

DUPLICATED SCENES

The book by echoing several passages in the two novels about nineteenth-century Missouri boys shows the kinds of scenes its writer enjoyed recording. In chapter VII, just as Huck has suffered from a nose that itches at an awkward time, Tom Canty suffers. In chapter XIII a sixteenth-century roisterer sings a song which the raftsmen have chanted in *Huck*, cleansed a bit, at Howells' suggestion, for juvenile readers. In chapter XVII a description is highly reminiscent of picturings of Huck and Jim alone on the river at night:

> All his sensations and experiences, as he moved through . . . the empty vastness of the night, were new and strange. . . . At intervals he heard voices approach, pass by, and fade into silence; and he saw nothing more of the bodies they belonged to than a sort of formless drifting blur. . . . Occasionally he caught a twinkle of light—always far away. . . . All sounds were remote; they made the little king feel . . . that he stood solitary, companionless, in the center of a measureless solitude.

In chapter XIX a woman tries, as Judith Loftus had, to identify a boyish visitor by asking shrewd questions; in chapter XX a demented hermit who believes himself an archangel tries to knife a boy, much as Pap, believing that Huck was the Angel of Death, had tried to kill his son.

TOM AND HUCK SHARE PREDICAMENTS

There are more important resemblances. Tom Canty, as the synopsis of the plot shows, is in the same fix as Huck Finn and Huck's creator: he is suffering from the restraints of "civilization," though—since the stuffy restraints of kingship are imposed upon him—his tortures are even worse.

Tom Canty is an amalgam of the characteristics of Huck Finn and Tom Sawyer. Like the former he is an unlearned child of poverty abused by a sadistic drunken father. Like the latter he is obsessed with imitating what he reads, and his gang join in acting out his reading: "Daily the mock prince," says chapter II, "was received with elaborate ceremonials borrowed . . . from his romantic readings . . . and daily his mimic highness issued decrees to his imaginary armies, navies, and vice-royalties." Like Tom Sawyer, Tom Canty enjoys sensational adventures and applause. The prince, though somewhat sketchily drawn, is blinded to reality in a Sawyerish way: Tom Canty unrealistically dreams of ceremonials; the prince unrealistically dreams of the free and easy life of the poor. As Tom Sawyer envies restraint-free Huck, the prince envies restraint-free Tom Canty.

COMMON CHARACTER TRAITS

Both boys have the innate goodness of heart that Tom and Huck have, and both, like Huck, oppose contemporaneous attitudes which they respect. Both demonstrate the truths which Clemens advocated in response to Lecky.[1] [British historian] David Hume's account of Edward, a historical source, quite possibly made Edward attractive to the author precisely because it indicated that he had this sort of internal conflict. Roger Blaine Salomon [in his classic *Twain and the Image of History*] has noticed that Hume saw Edward as combining "mildness of disposition . . . and an attachment to equity and justice" with tendencies toward "bigotry and persecution" which he "seems only to have contracted from his education, and from the age in which he lived." At the outset of the story, in chapter III, Edward shows his innate benevolence by sympathizing with Tom Canty; at the conclusion, having learned at first hand about unjust laws, he shows it by ruling benevolently. In chapter XV Tom Canty as the bogus king, on hearing that a man, a woman, and a young girl have been condemned to death for crimes against the realm, has these thoughts:

> Death—and violent death—for those poor unfortunates! The thought wrung Tom's heartstrings. The spirit of compassion took control of him, to the exclusion of all other considerations; he never thought of the offended laws, or of the grief or loss which these three criminals had inflicted upon their victims; he would think of nothing but . . . the grisly fate hanging over the heads of the condemned.

Here is a sixteenth-century parallel for Huck's helping Jim escape from slavery despite his having been taught that such an act is sinful. The kindness of heart, Salomon notices, is in each instance an attribute of childhood. The idea is reiterated in chapter XIX, when Edward, sleeping in rags in a barn, awakens to find two children "staring with innocent eyes" at him. When he tells them that he is the king, unlike adults they instinctively believe him. Similarly, in chapter XXV, when all appearances are against the truth of a claim made by the king's traveling companion, Miles Hendon, " 'I do not doubt thee,' says the king, with a childlike simplicity and faith." Miles, an adult, by contrast does doubt Edward's legal claims. "Children and fools," Clemens remarked in a notebook about the time he set down this incident, "*always* speak truth."

These encounters occur while Edward is journeying

---

1. William Hartpole Lecky's *History of European Morale* had a major influence on the evolution of Twain's philosophy on human nature.

across country. During much of the journey he is accompanied by Miles, who, although he does not believe that the ragged youngster is the king, humors him by waiting on him and by pretending to believe that honors the boy bestows upon him are real—"a most odd and strange position, truly," he muses in chapter XII, "for one so matter-of-fact as I." As this remark suggests, Hendon is to the king what Huck has been to Tom—Sancho Panza to Don Quixote, and the journey is a sixteenth-century counterpart of the nineteenth-century journey of Huck and Jim.

ON CONSCIENCE

Not only does Mark Twain repeat in this fiction his beliefs about instinctive goodness; he also repeats his ideas—and Lecky's—about a bedeviling conscience. In chapter XXX Tom Canty suffers severe pangs because he remembers his injustice to Edward. In chapter XXXI he suffers similarly when he has denied recognizing his mother. Twain also shows characters deriving selfish pleasure from virtuous actions. In chapter XIX, after a peasant woman and Edward have exchanged kindnesses: "This good woman was made happy all day by the applauses she got of herself for her magnanimous condescension to a tramp; and the king was just as self-complacent over his gracious humility toward a humble peasant woman." For childish readers who derive a moral from their reading, the author affixes one: "It does us all good to unbend some times." All the points except that made in the moralizing sentence—an ironic one—are reiterations of observations already made in *Huck*.

COMMON PHILOSOPHICAL BASIS

Gladys Bellamy, in [*Mark Twain as a Literary Artist*] her study of Mark Twain's thought, calls attention to a final point made in this novel that repeats a concept already developed in *Huck* and to be developed there again. She sees *The Prince and the Pauper* as

> Mark Twain's first full-length study of the power of determining environment and circumstance. The transformation of beggar into prince and vice versa was effected by a mere change of clothes. The significance of clothes . . . rests upon some such explanation as this: since the world judges by outward appearance, the clothes one wears become a part of the exterior determining circumstances which decide what everyone will be. . . . Mark Twain gave . . . his attention to the

> pressure of environment upon the moral fiber . . . of Tom
> Canty. . . . Tom lapses from a sturdy rebellion . . . into sloth-
> ful enjoyment of the splendors that surround him. Finally he
> sinks into a corrupt resignation. . . .

Though I have, perhaps rather impolitely, omitted a few commentaries of Miss Bellamy's with which I do not agree, and though I believe that Tom—since he is endowed with a good heart—never becomes as corrupt as she indicates, I am convinced that in general Miss Bellamy's analysis is sound. Here as elsewhere Twain is conducting the discussion with Lecky which he had begun in *Huckleberry Finn* and which he resumed in later parts of that novel.

When, however, we make a distinction between the journey of Huck and Jim recounted in chapters of *Huck* written in 1876 and that recounted in the portions written later, we see that *The Prince and the Pauper* foreshadows important developments.

The little king during his wanderings meets criminals and confidence men; he is taken to be a vagrant who is pretending to be of royal blood. The king and the duke in *Huck* are vagrant confidence men who pretend that they are of noble and royal descent. Despite the fact that they disbelieve Edward's claims, the boys at Christ hospital, the Canty family, Miles Hendon, and the band of beggars and robbers all humor Edward by addressing him as royalty and bowing to him. Hendon calls him "my liege," serves him, and helps him dress. In chapter XIX of *Huck* the duke "said we ought to bow when we spoke to him, and say 'Your Grace,' or 'Your Lordship' . . . and one of us ought to wait on him. . . ." The bogus dauphin "said it made him feel easier and better for a while if people treated him according to his rights and got down on one knee to speak to him, and always called him 'Your Majesty,' and waited on him first. . . ." Huck comments:

> It didn't take me long to make up my mind that these liars
> warn't no kings nor dukes at all, but just low-down humbugs
> and frauds. But I . . . kept it to myself; it's the best way; then
> you don't have no quarrels, and don't get in no trouble. If they
> wanted us to call them kings and dukes, I hadn't no objec-
> tions, 'long as it would keep peace. . . .

The characters in *The Prince and the Pauper* defer to what they consider a whim for purposes of mockery or because of kindness; Huck defers because of his habit of generating as little friction as possible. Yet the essentially similar situations seemed to Twain to be good literary material.

These are foreshadowings of situations to be embodied in *Huck* when Mark returned to it. Far above these in importance are foreshadowings of a whole line of action and important related themes.

SHARED THEMES AND PLOT LINES

In his letter to [the eminent U.S. writer and editor William Dean] Howells outlining the plot of *The Prince and the Pauper* the author said:

> My idea is to afford a realizing sense of the exceeding severity of the laws of that day by inflicting some of the penalties upon the King himself and allowing him a chance to see the rest of them applied to others—all of which is to account for certain mildnesses which distinguish Edward VI's reign from those that preceded and followed it.

Considered with the author's outline of his plot, this suggests an interrelationship between happenings and a theme: Edward "has a rough time amongst tramps and ruffians"; some penalties of the day are inflicted upon him and he sees others applied to his people. Because he thus acquires "a realizing sense" of the harsh laws, when he returns to his throne he becomes a mild ruler. The novel is so patterned. After seeing and personally experiencing sundry injustices, Edward, restored to his throne, rights injustices in a crammed final chapter. "The world is made wrong," he moralizes; "kings should go to school to their own laws at times and so learn mercy."

The Prince and the Pauper has relationships with Mark's previous stories of educational journeyings in which each character loses his romantic conception of a sort of life, and each learns the actualities of that sort of life—Tom Canty, the life of the court; Edward, the life of his subjects.

It is Edward's encounters on his journeyings which enlarge his understanding. These are with people of many sorts—outcasts who have no excuse for their lawlessness but who prey upon others; well-intentioned folk who have been driven to lawbreaking because they have suffered unjustly; victims of injustice. In chapter XXVII, when Edward sees two Baptist women burned at the stake for their faith while their horrified children watch, his comments show how deeply he is shaken:

> The king glanced from the frantic girls to the stake, then turned his ashen face to the wall, and looked no more. He said: "That which I have seen, in that one little moment, will

never go out from my memory, but will abide there; and I
shall see it all the days, and dream of it all the nights, till I die.
Would God I had been blind!'"

In chapters of *Huckleberry Finn* written about this time or
soon after, the nineteenth-century ragamuffin, like the sixteenth-century king in rags, on a journey encounters many
sorts of men and women. He, too, has harrowing encounters
with human depravity and cruelty. He, too, watches a mani-
festation of human brutality (chapter XVIII) so horrible that
it sears his memory:

> It made me so sick I almost fell out of the tree. I ain't a-going
> to tell *all* that happened—it would make me sick again if I
> was to do that. I wished I hadn't ever come ashore that night
> to see those things. I ain't ever going to get shut of them—lots
> of times I dream about them.

The differences in language do not conceal the essential
identity in content of the two passages.

Mob Violence Demonstrative of Human Nature

In both instances, although the boys are horrified by the violence of the crowd, something other than mob violence is
involved. But noteworthy in *The Prince and the Pauper* is the
picturing of many mobs in action—often violent action. In
chapter III a mob at the gate to Westminster jeers at Tom,
grovels when the prince rebukes them, then maltreats Edward when he reappears in Tom's rags. In chapter X a priest
who comes to Tom's defense when another mob bedevils
him is struck down and: "The mob pressed on, their enjoyment nothing disturbed." In chapter XI, when a mob sees
Edward attempting to enter the Guildhall, they "taunt and
mock him." When Hendon comes to his aid "a score of
voices shouted 'Kill the dog! kill him! kill him!'" and he
barely misses being destroyed. In chapter XIV a sadistic mob
eagerly surges forward to watch an execution. In chapter
XXVIII a mob is impressed into silence by Hendon's bravery,
and in chapter XXXII a mob demonstrates its fickleness by
siding alternately with Tom and with Edward.

There are similar representations of mobs as fickle, cruel,
and cowardly in the new chapters of *Huck.* There, too, the
mobs shift rapidly, backing one force and then another; they
gloat as they watch human suffering; they overwhelm and
torture their victims; they slink away when faced by a brave
man. . . . Details about these Mississippi River mobs, like

those about mobs in the historical romance, were inspired largely by reading about mobs active during the French Revolution. And the depiction of these frantic groups was to enable Mark Twain, in *Huck*, to say important things about man's nature.

The author, I suggest, hit upon the scheme of most of the rest of *Huckleberry Finn* in part as a result of his working with similar lines of action in his historical novel.

CONCLUSIONS DIFFER

The essential meanings of the novels are, to be sure, different in important respects. The injustices which the king discovers are injustices in the England of his day, and the implication is that a just king will remedy them. Huck observes, specifically, the injustice, the cruelty, the hypocrisy, of the ante-bellum Southwest; but the author's condemnation is broadened to include not simply Southerners but all humanity; and the implication is that the tendencies are innate and beyond eradication. Nevertheless, I suggest that Mark Twain learned a great deal about ways to develop this theme as he wrote his novel for children.

Twain's View of History in His Major Novels

By Roger Salomon

In *Twain and the Image of History*, Roger Salomon of the University of California, analyzes Mark Twain's view of historical progress as it evolved through his major novels. In his earlier work, *Life on the Mississippi*, Twain embraced the historical process. He believed that the human character was the result of the influences of heredity and the environment and that the former factor stayed constant while the latter improved through progress. Human perfection could be achieved through the steady improvement in political and social institutions and the correct moral training. In his later fiction, however, beginning with *The Prince and the Pauper*, his growing pessimism and belief that every institution had its own set of evils which would ultimately corrupt the human spirit, were predominant. In the following extract Salomon says that while *The Prince and the Pauper* presented a strong case for progress through education, it also contained the major themes, symbols, and images of his later novels which suggested that society inevitably destroys the innate goodness of children. According to Salomon, Mark Twain came to view the historical process as a cyclical and endless return of evil.

The Prince and the Pauper [is] an early result of the same intellectual ferment that produced *Life on the Mississippi, Huckleberry Finn,* and eventually *A Connecticut Yankee*. It is a book which closely reflects the themes, imagery, and much of the subject matter of these three other artistically greater works. In *The Prince and the Pauper* are the same attacks on feudalism and false romance, the same hatred of

Excerpted from *Twain and the Image of History*, by Roger Salomon. Copyright © 1957 by Roger Salomon and the Mark Twain Company. Reprinted with permission from Yale University Press.

mobs and small town provincialism, the same generally pessimistic picture of human nature, and the same appeal to the natural goodness of children. Tom Canty and his counterpart Prince Edward are amalgamations of the characters of Tom Sawyer and Huckleberry Finn; their vision is clouded and distorted by false romanticism as the story begins, but they learn from their suffering to see life clearly and honestly for what it is—to see (using Twain's metaphor in *Life on the Mississippi)* the snags beneath the picturesque surface of the river. Tom Canty comes from essentially the same poor and depraved background as Huck; both have cruel and drunken fathers who are killed or disappear; both (this time with Prince Edward as Tom) make friends and take up with fellow outcasts and victims of injustice; and both take representative tours through society. Altogether *The Prince and the Pauper* is a significant enough book to warrant our taking a closer look at it than it has hitherto received.

PARALLELS WITH *A CONNECTICUT YANKEE*

In its official theme *The Prince and the Pauper* bears close resemblance to *A Connecticut Yankee.* "My idea," Twain wrote [author and editor William Dean] Howells during the later stages of its composition,

> is to afford a realizing sense of the exceeding severity of the laws of that day by inflicting some of their penalties upon the King himself and allowing him a chance to see the rest of them applied to others—all of which is to account for certain mildnesses which distinguished Edward VI's reign from those that preceded and followed it.

Just as in the *Yankee,* Twain's treatment of these laws in *The Prince and the Pauper* is frankly anachronistic; both books are compendiums of the worst features of English and European social legislation from the sixth to the nineteenth century (though the latter makes more of a passing bow to verisimilitude).

In his original preface to the *Yankee,* Twain specifically discusses the Connecticut Blue Laws and points out that they were milder than English legislation of the same period: "There was never a time when America applied the death-penalty to more than fourteen crimes. But England, within the memory of men still living, had in her list of crimes 223 which were punishable by death." This passage closely parallels a paragraph in his "General Note" at the end of *The Prince and the Pauper:* "There has never been a time—under the Blue-Laws or any other—when above FOURTEEN crimes were punishable by death in Connecticut. But in England, within the memory of men who are still hale in body and mind, TWO HUNDRED AND TWENTY-THREE crimes were punishable by death!" The similarity here is so striking as to suggest not only the identical impulse behind the two books but also that Twain, in writing the *Yankee,* must have re-examined *The Prince and the Pauper* and the historical materials used in this book. In his own list of the sources of *A Connecticut Yankee* Twain lists Trumbull's *Blue Laws, True and False.* Perhaps another result of this re-examination is the use of almost identical plot devices for revealing the enormity of social injustice: in both books, the kings inadvertently become wandering outcasts and are forced to "go to school to their own laws" in order to "learn mercy"—the words are Edward's and express his revelation and his hope.

EDWARD LEARNS MERCY

Edward and Arthur are noble and courageous individuals, who tower above the craven and persecuting mobs which are always nipping at their heels. But only Edward "learns mercy," and he "learns" it only because he can still instinctively respond to human suffering. Arthur, great as he is in his own way (as the Yankee comes to recognize), can only respond to the demands of his own code. When he remains in the smallpox hut, for example, he does so, Twain stresses, primarily because he "considered his knightly honor at stake." Not that Arthur is without feelings of pity in this scene; the point is simply that his first and primary response is always (to use Twain's dichotomy) to his "moral sense" rather than his "heart." On another occasion he tells the Yankee that "his conscience . . . was troubling him" because he had encountered two young men escaping from their cruel lord and was doing nothing to catch them and turn them in. Subsequently, he urges on the mob after these men and refuses to cut down a hanged (but apparently still living) man from a tree because, as he puts it, "if he hanged himself, he was willing to lose his property to his lord; so let him be. If others hanged him, belike they had the right—let him hang."

These are responses which move within the narrow limitations of what Twain considered to be a medieval and aristo-

cratic code of conduct, and their contrast with those of both
Edward and Huck Finn in similar situations is obvious and
startling. *Adult* kings apparently can not "learn mercy" by
going "to school to their own laws." The Yankee castigates
Arthur in terms more concrete but, nevertheless, similar in
tone to those he had used earlier on the vicious Morgan le Fay:

> He could see only one side of it [i.e. the debate on whether or
> not to try to catch the escaped peasants]. He was born so, ed-
> ucated so, his veins were full of ancestral blood that was rot-
> ten with this sort of unconscious brutality, brought down by
> inheritance from a long procession of hearts that had each
> done its share toward poisoning the stream.

The escape of these men, subject, as they were, to the will
and pleasure of their lord, was an insult and outrage, "a
thing not to be countenanced by any conscientious person
who knew his duty to his sacred caste." On the king, in other
words, lay the full burden of the Fall [the first corruption of
Adam and Eve]. Beyond any hope of redemption he was
cursed with the moral sense—that curious concept which in
Twain's hands really becomes an attempt (evident enough
in the above passage) to describe the influence, not only of
one's immediate environment, but of what [American author William] Faulkner has aptly called the "entailed birthright" of the past. Clearly Arthur could not himself amelio-
rate a society which, even before he was born, had already
claimed him as its most important victim. Only a deus ex
machina, an external force which presumably represented
"better" environmental training, could effect changes. Significantly, however, the Yankee's changes are burlesqued,
shunted into the background, and finally wiped out, while
Twain keeps a steady focus on the spectacle of human suffering and human inertia caused by the moral sense. In *A
Connecticut Yankee* Twain put his entire faith in progress
and that faith wavered badly. "There are times," admits the
Yankee at one point, "when one would like to hang the
whole human race and finish the farce."

INNOCENCE CONFRONTS INJUSTICE

In *The Prince and the Pauper*, on the other hand, Twain
combined his official theme of Whig progressivism with the
dream of innate goodness which, during this time, was so
integral a part of his image of childhood. The book contains
the same kind of duality of values [as those found] in *Life on*

the Mississippi, but in *The Prince and the Pauper* there is less sense of potential disparity because the antisocial values are used for social ends. In a fairy story (and only there) Tom Canty masquerading as an absolute monarch could achieve the kind of omnipotence that allowed him magically to set things right in society before society destroyed the goodness he was born with. The reign of Edward VI was, of course, an ideal vehicle for Twain's purposes. Not only had the Somerset protectorate [the governing officials during the boy-king's reign], with its firm Protestantism and its retreat from the pure absolutism of Henry VIII, received the seal of approval of the Whig historians, but also, and more important, the alleged personal qualities of the boy king were those to which Twain was sure to respond. "How his name shines out of the midst of that long darkness," he once wrote, at the same time arguing that Edward was the only good English ruler before Victoria. The tone of this comment is close to that which Twain used normally when talking about Joan of Arc and suggests how much Joan was simply a feminized and somewhat more grown-up Edward. Both (in contrast to Arthur) were miraculous exceptions to all the laws of history as Twain conceived them, yet individuals who had somehow made an impact on history—individuals who at least had managed to illuminate the darkness briefly with their own innocence. They were logically impossible, as Twain's contrasting treatment of Arthur makes only too clear, but in their very impossibility lay their goodness, and in their goodness lay all the goodness of history. In *The Prince and the Pauper* Twain would "account for certain mildnesses which distinguished Edward VI's reign from those that preceded and followed it," not by an appeal to institutions as he did later in *A Connecticut Yankee,* but by bringing innate goodness directly to bear on iniquity.

HISTORICAL ACCURACY OF EDWARD'S CHARACTER

In the working out of this theme, only the career of Joan of Arc would furnish Twain more ready-made raw materials— more of those historical "facts" he so cherished—than did the short life of Edward VI. David Hume, Twain's chief historical source, describes Edward as possessing "mildness of disposition, application to study and business, a capacity to learn and judge, and an attachment to equity and justice." Hume adds only one qualifier: "He seems only to have contracted, from his education, and from the age in which he lived, too much of a narrow predisposition in matters of religion, which made him incline somewhat to bigotry and persecution." In the personality of Edward VI, in short, a good heart was in conflict with a stultifying conscience. In an earlier passage Hume gives a telling illustration of this conflict. A young woman called Joan Bocher was about to be sent to the stake on an obscure point of heresy until young Edward, who "had more sense than all his counsellors and preceptors," intervened and "refused to sign the warrant for her execution." Only after all sorts of weighty theological arguments were brought to bear on him did he submit, "though with tears in his eyes."

TOM'S COMPASSION

Here, indeed, was material aplenty for Twain. In *The Prince and the Pauper* he apparently echoes Hume in that scene in which Tom Canty as Edward first really asserts his new and fortuitously won power. Inquiring about a hooting and shouting mob approaching along the road—the mob, here as elsewhere, Twain's most effective symbol of the craven baseness of most human beings—Tom is informed that they are following a man, woman, and young girl to execution. His reaction is immediate and instinctive: "The spirit of compassion took control of him, to the exclusion of all other considerations; he never thought of the offended laws, or of the grief or loss which these criminals had inflicted upon their victims, he could think of nothing but the scaffold and the grisly fate hanging over the heads of the condemned." This, incidentally, is a paler but more explicit statement of Huck's feelings when he sees the king and duke tarred and feathered: "Well, it made me sick to see it, and I was sorry for them poor pitiful rascals, it seemed like I couldn't even feel any hardness against them any more in the world. It was a dreadful thing to see. Human beings *can* be awful cruel to one another." But, where Tom can intervene and set right, Huck can only look on and mourn; this is the truest measure of the maturity of the later book.

Before Tom does set things right, however, he almost turns the condemned over to their fate because the evidence of witchcraft against them seems overwhelming and because his mind (again like Huck's) completely accepts the superstitions of his day. Only at the last instant does he save them by the native shrewdness of his questioning—a product, not of his learning, but of his lack of education mingled with his strong grasp of empiric reality and his innate sense of values. These are the same kind of questions which Twain enjoyed putting in the mouth of Nigger Jim and which (when Twain uses the technique for something more than its mechanical joke value) undercut so effectively the dogmas of society.

TWAIN'S THEORY OF PROGRESS

Edward VI, of course, as befitted a monarch who was to have no parallel before the later nineteenth century, was conceived of by Twain and his sources as a great believer in education. After he has been set upon and beaten by the boys of Christ's Hospital, he resolves that, when he regains power,

> they shall not have bread and shelter only, but also teachings out of books; for a full belly is little worth where the mind's starved, and the heart. I will keep this diligently in my remembrance, that this day's lesson be not lost upon me, and my people suffer thereby; for learning softeneth the heart and breedeth gentleness and charity.

Edward's sentiments here have a certain amount of historical accuracy (as Twain was quick to point out) and what is more important, are completely in accord with Twain's theory of progress. However, it is hard to believe that Edward could have perpetuated these sentiments after his subsequent experiences along the road—all of which seem to point a different moral.

At the height of Edward's degradation, for example, when he has escaped from the gang of thieves and is walking the roads ragged, lonely, and hungry, he meets rebuffs and curses every time he stops at a farmhouse and asks for help. With a sense of total isolation from the rest of humanity, he stumbles along the road. "All sounds were remote; they made the little king feel that all life and activity were far removed from him, and that he stood solitary, companionless, in the center of a measureless solitude." He finally slips unnoticed into a barn and lies down next to something he soon discovers is a calf. "The king was not only delighted to find that the creature was only a calf," Twain wrote,

> but delighted to have the calf's company; for he had been feeling so lonesome and friendless that the company and comradeship of even this humble animal was welcome. And he had been so buffeted, so rudely entreated by his own kind, that

it was a real comfort to him to feel that he was at last in the society of a fellow creature that had at least a soft heart and a
gentle spirit, whatever loftier attributes might be lacking. So he
resolved to waive rank and make friends with the calf.

This association of boy and calf—of a child uncorrupted by
civilization with a creature beyond its pale—is reminiscent
of both the relationship of Huck and Jim and Eve and the animals in Eden. This relationship is the "divine estate" that
Satan described to Eve when he told her that whatever she
and the animals did was "right and innocent."

Characteristically, Twain's image of man before the Fall is
quickly followed by the complementary image of sleep and
stasis. After Edward has cuddled up to the calf,

pleasant thoughts came at once; life took on a cheerfuler
seeming. He was free of the bonds of servitude and crime,
free of the companionship of base and brutal criminals; he
was warm, he was sheltered; in a word, he was happy. The
night wind . . . swept by in fitful gusts. . . . He merely snug-
gled the closer to his friend in a luxury of warm contentment
and drifted blissfully out of consciousness into a deep and
dreamless sleep that was full of serenity and peace.

Youth and Sleep as Major Symbols

Youth, innocence, freedom, and sleep—these ideas and images were inextricably mingled in Twain's consciousness to
suggest a mode of existence far removed from the terrors of
time and history. That they were somehow related to personal
psychological problems seems obvious. He once commented
in a revealing note: "I was never old in a dream yet." As major symbols, youth and sleep lie at the very center of Twain's
best fiction. Where Edward achieves a momentary freedom
with the calf in a barn, Huck flees from the Grangerford feud
to Jim and the raft, but the pattern remains the same. "You
feel mighty free and easy and comfortable on a raft," says
Huck, and there follows an idyll of three days and nights as
they drift down the river, go naked (clothes, of course, being
one of the prime symbols in the book of the civilization Huck
is rejecting), and "watch the lonesomeness of the river, and
kind of lazy along and by and by lazy off to sleep." For Huck,
"other places do seem so cramped up and smothery, but a raft
don't." The reference to places "cramped up and smothery" is
another image of civilization like that of clothes: i.e. houses,
institutions, and, by extension, the entire system of rigid determinism which constitutes for Twain the "law" of history.

ADULTS LOSE HONEST INSTINCTS

When King Edward awakes on the following morning, he finds himself being stared at by two little girls "with their innocent eyes." Almost without question, they accept his pledge that he is king, and he, in turn, pours out his troubles "where they would not be scoffed at or doubted." Eventually they run to get him food, and the king says to himself:

> When I am come to mine own again, I will always honor little children, remembering how that these trusted me and believed in me in my time of trouble; whilst they that were older, and thought themselves wiser, mocked at me and held me for a liar.

Twain hammers home this point with particular force when the children's mother receives Edward kindly but pities his "apparently crazed intellect." Even the best and most sympathetic of adults, in short (and these were few and far between), had lost the innocence, the instinctive—and, to the adult, naive—honesty that they were born with. Later in the novel, when Miles Hendon himself is accused of being an impostor, he asks the king if he doubts him, and the king answers immediately, "with a childlike simplicity and faith," that he does not. But to Edward's own question, "dost thou doubt me?" Hendon, the adult, can give no such simple and spontaneous answer.

HOPE AND DESPAIR IN TWAIN'S VIEW OF HISTORY

"I have never written a book for boys; I write for grown ups who have *been* boys," Twain noted late in life. His distinction is a crucial one. The importance of boyhood, Twain seems to be saying, lies not so much in the kind of experiences encountered, as in the way a boy reacts to experience—a way which reflects a complex of values enormously precious to the mature person but undiscoverable in the adult world of time and history. The children who befriended Edward, and Edward himself, were as yet almost unmarred by the knowledge of good and evil which would be an inevitable part of their later development. Perhaps the growth of reason would compensate for the loss of innocence and bring about a Utopia greater than the one that had been lost; this has been the dominant hope of Western Society at least since the seventeenth century, a hope predicated squarely on the acceptance of history. With a part of his consciousness Twain, of course, embraced this hope. His Edward, as we have already noted, plans to educate the children of Christ's Hospital, for "learning softeneth the heart and breedeth gentleness and charity." But that part of Twain which rejected the ameliorative influence of history—which, in other words, could no longer accept the theory that history was the vehicle carrying man forward to the new Eden—necessarily rejected all hope.

THE ENDLESS RETURN OF EVIL

Individuals of most earlier societies could dream of Eden without predicating their dreams on the forward movement of history. For the ancients the future was the past: Eden would return and then decay again during an infinity of cycles, a more or less mechanical process which, for all practical purposes, annulled time and "abolished" history. Such cyclical theories were essentially optimistic. Catastrophe was normal and certain in meaning because no event was irreversible, no transformation final. For the Western mind, however, nurtured on the concept of one great cycle of Fall and Redemption, cyclical theories (especially as they have been secularized in modern times from cycles of cosmos to those of civilization—not "abolishing" history but simply making it meaningless) are an expression of pessimism and hopelessness. Certainly they are for Twain, who stresses the endless return of evil—never of Eden. There was only one Eden and that was in the past—in dreams, in fantasy, in the responses of children, in the image of a raft floating down the Mississippi.

The "Unpromising Hero" Tales

Robert Regan

In the following extract from *Unpromising Heroes: Mark Twain and His Characters*, author Robert Regan says that in *The Prince and the Pauper* Mark Twain dealt successfully with two of his most conflicting desires, his wish to succeed in the world and yet be free to be his own person. He managed this reconciliation, connecting the virtues of Tom Sawyer and Huckleberry Finn, by using what Regan calls the "unpromising hero motif" in the characters of Tom Canty, Prince Edward, and Miles Hendon. Regan defines "unpromising hero" as "an unlikely youngster who, against all odds and every expectation, wins his way to success in the world." In *The Prince and the Pauper,* Regan notes three major elements that are characteristic of unpromising hero tales and serve to unify the novel.

At the last possible moment in *The Adventures of Tom Sawyer,* Tom and Huck make a kind of pact: Tom will let Huck into his "high-toned" robber gang and Huck will give the civilized life another try. That pact constituted a victory for Tom, and a kind of victory for Mark Twain also, for it forged a link between the two boys who embodied their creator's deepest wishes—Tom, the wish to succeed; Huck, the wish to be free, to be his own man. But the link, as every reader knows, as Mark Twain himself must have known, would not hold: Tom was irrevocably committed to that journey to law school via West Point which Judge Thatcher had promised to arrange for him, and Huck was equally, if less consciously, committed to a journey in an opposite direction, a journey toward the freedom represented by the Territory. The two boys could not remain themselves and remain together for long. Whatever the

achievements of *The Adventures of Tom Sawyer,* it failed to effect a permanent rapprochement between the fantasy of success and the dream of independence. Mark Twain's next
novel, in happy contrast, proved a notable success on that
score. In *The Prince and the Pauper* (1882) Mark Twain found
a new and more effective way of coping with the challenge of
accommodating the Tom Sawyer Impulse and the Huck Finn
Impulse: he presented three heroes—two of them boys, the
third an adult who had not outgrown the innocent strength of
boyhood—and in each of these characters he linked the special virtue of Tom with that of Huck.

Roger B. Salomon has observed [in his *Mark Twain and
the Image of History*] that both of the two boy heroes of the
novel combine attributes of Tom Sawyer and Huck Finn, and
that they both progress from a vision of life typical of Tom toward one typical of Huck:

> Tom Canty and his counterpart Prince Edward are amalga-
> mations of the characters of Tom Sawyer and Huckleberry
> Finn; their vision is clouded and distorted by false romanti-
> cism as the story begins, but they learn from their suffering
> to see life clearly and honestly for what it is. . . .

There are many other ways in which Prince Edward and his
pauper-double, Tom Canty, combine characteristics of the
two boys in the earlier novel. Some of these will appear as we
examine both Prince and Pauper as Unpromising Heroes.

QUEST FOR IDENTITY

Our first glimpse of Tom Canty indicates the kind of role he is
to play. On the day of his birth, all England was talking joyfully
about another newborn babe, the Prince of Wales, Edward
Tudor, "but there was no talk about . . . Tom Canty, lapped in
his poor rags, except among the family of paupers he had just
come to trouble with his presence." In spite of his poverty, and
because of it, Tom dreams of the life of a prince—"the
charmed life of a petted prince in a royal palace." But Mark
Twain is at pains to make Tom a modest child, even in his
fantasies: he dreams not of being a prince but of merely *seeing* one. When he confides his self-effacing dreams of glory
to some of his comrades, they jeer him and scoff at him;
thereafter he keeps his dreams to himself. Hidden from the
world, his fantasies work all the more strongly upon his
mind and he begins to speak like a prince and act the prince.
At first this amuses his playmates, but their amusement

gradually changes to admiration and the admiration spreads from the children of Offal Court, Tom's residence, to the adults. These begin to bring their problems to the princely pauper for solution, and acting the part of the young Jesus among the doctors, he astonishes them with "the wit and wisdom of his decisions." Becoming a little more like Tom Sawyer, Tom Canty next organizes a royal court in which he plays the prince and his playmates the attendant lords and ladies. All of this prepares the pauper, and the reader, for the great change in his life, his trading places, quite inadvertently, with Edward, Prince of Wales. Tom Canty's response to the transformation of his identity is the antithesis of what we would expect from a Tom Sawyer: mistaken for the prince, he tries his best to convince the royal court that he is an unwitting imposter. But no one will believe his protestations; the courtiers and even the dying King Henry mistake the truth Tom tries to tell them for an insane delusion. The Prince, they believe, has gone quite mad; he has suffered, they are convinced, the ultimate alienation, the loss of his sense of self. Just as Huck Finn would accommodate himself to the identity thrust upon him at Phelps farm, the little pauper adjusts to his situation and accepts for as long as he must the fantastic misunderstanding everyone else takes for the truth: if they insist he is the heir apparent—and presently the king—he will play the role. Note, however, that Tom Canty takes his place at the head of the authority-structure without adopting the folkways of the authority-structure. All of his acts as king strike at the cruelty, prejudice, and ignorance upon which, in Mark Twain's view, the crown based its power. For as long as he reigns, he enjoys Tom Sawyer's success without paying Tom Sawyer's price.

Parallel Journeys

Prince Edward's case is superficially Tom Canty's turned upside down, but actually it is not reversed at all. The mistake in identities thrusts Edward into the pauper's place; suddenly translated from the Palace to Offal Court, he becomes what the other boy had been before, a ragged wanderer who talks like a prince and dreams of the life of a prince. His road from Offal Court to Westminster Abbey is longer and harder than Tom Canty's, but it leads in the same direction and passes the same landmarks. Each boy must make his way through jeering, scoffing mobs: each must have his identity and his sanity challenged by both the hostile and the hospitable people he meets in his travels; each must witness along his way terrible spectacles of man's inhumanity to man, just as Huck Finn would witness one horror after another during his journey down the river. In another significant respect Prince Edward is identified with Tom Canty: he too re-enacts a notable scene in the life of Christ. Just as the Roman soldiers stripped Jesus "and put on him a scarlet robe . . . and platted a crown of thorns . . . [and] put it upon his head, and a reed in his right hand; and they bowed the knee before him and mocked him saying, Hail King of the Jews," so the band of beggars and criminals Edward falls among robe and scepter and crown him:

> Almost before the poor little victim could draw a breath he was crowned with a tin basin, robed in a tattered blanket, throned upon a barrel, and sceptered with the tinker's soldering-iron. Then all flung themselves upon their knees about him and sent up a chorus of ironical wailings, and mocking supplications, while they swabbed their eyes with their soiled and ragged sleeves and aprons.

The portion of the life of Christ which Tom Canty had reenacted was, in keeping with the difference of treatment Mark Twain gives the two boys, a much happier one. Edward, who is being educated for a higher office than Tom is to occupy, is appropriately made to suffer more pathetic humiliations. After his long journey through the "underworld" of his kingdom and a long night's sleep in the tomb of King Edward the Confessor, those humiliations ultimate in the coronation scene, a kind of ritual resurrection from the dead.

MILES HENDON AS UNPROMISING HERO

Tom Canty and Prince Edward are not the only Unpromising Heroes in the novel: the Prince's protector, Miles Hendon, is in more details than either of the boys a member of that class. Miles's troubles begin in sibling rivalry. He is, like Samuel Clemens, a middle brother near in age to the youngest. His younger brother, Hugh, is the tattletale, spoilsport Sid Sawyer grown up, "a mean spirit, covetous, treacherous, vicious, underhanded—a reptile." He has caused Miles to be sent into virtual exile; and their father and the eldest brother having died during his years of exile, the treacherous Hugh has possessed himself of Miles's inheritance and married his sweetheart.

For Mark Twain the greatest difficulty in presenting an Unpromising Hero tale seriously (i.e., melodramatically, not satirically) lay in making the hero succeed *without* trying: if the hero seems to be seeking his own advancement we lose sympathy with him. This is, in part, what shook our confidence in Tom Sawyer in the earlier novel; it is what was to reduce Tom to something of a comic butt in the opening of *Tom Sawyer Abroad,* and . . . Mark Twain [took] pains to avoid it in his later novels. . . .

Miles Hendon's story solves the problem ingeniously. Long before Miles learns that his brother has cheated him of everything which is by rights his, he meets the pathetic young prince who has been driven in a pauper's rags from the palace. He has little inkling of the similarity of their predicaments, but he takes the seemingly mad boy under his protection and saves him from a bloodthirsty mob. Moments later we learn that Henry VIII is dead: the lad Miles has saved from death is England's rightful king. He will in due time create his protector Earl of Kent and bestow upon him unique dignities as reward for the services he renders him. But Miles does not render those services to the king; rather he champions and serves a mad beggar-boy helpless to care for himself. Miles's exertions on behalf of Edward are as selfless as Huck's on behalf of Jim: he has nothing whatever to gain except jeers and hoots and a dozen lashes. The fable is perfectly contrived to allow Hendon to succeed without trying.

EDWARD AND TOM AS UNPROMISING HEROES

The fable is equally successful in dealing with this pitfall of the Unpromising Hero motif in the cases of Edward and Tom. Edward is of course above suspicion: since all power and honor are his by right of birth he cannot be accused of seeking either; but the novel reinforces the point by making power and honor his by right of suffering and sympathy also. Tom Canty is exonerated of any charge of seeking his own advancement since he repeatedly attempts to escape from the captivity of kingship by protesting that he is not Edward Tudor. He even dreams of being back in Offal Court, a pauper joyful in the possession of twelve pennies. Although Tom's essential goodness of heart is never in question, he wavers in his honesty to himself at a crucial moment in the action. When he first resigns himself to playing the king's part, he thinks at once of his mother and wonders if he could make her Duchess of Offal Court, but she gradually fades from his mind. On the day of the coronation, she sees him and recognizes him; he denies her, in words which again sound a biblical echo: "I do not know you, woman." Life in the court, this failure of Tom's moral integrity seems to say, can corrupt even the purest, the most innocent will. But remorse follows at once; the confrontation with his mother recalls to Tom his earlier insight that his royal state is in actuality a kind of slavery and he exclaims to himself, "Would God I were free of my captivity." The incident assures his making the right choice when the true king appears in rags at the coronation and claims his crown. But Tom Canty, in common with King Edward VI and Miles, Earl of Kent, is an Unpromising Hero, and his honest acknowledgement of the true king must not deprive him of the success which is his due: Tom, who had ironically been called "the little Prince of Pauperdom" in an early scene, becomes, appropriately, a kind of king of paupers, the chief governor of Christ's Hospital. Edward's gesture in giving Tom that place makes a fit conclusion not only to Tom's history but to his own also: the boys of Christ's Hospital had abused their prince shamefully when he was in pauper's rags and Tom Canty had, however unwillingly, usurped the place of the rightful king for a season; yet when Edward regains his throne, instead of punishing the boys of Christ's Hospital and the usurper, he rewards both: he places his alter-ego over the charity boys in order to ensure that they "shall have their minds and hearts fed, as well as their baser parts." The young king proves by that enlightened and merciful act that his long educational journey has brought him to its destination.

SHARED FATHER FIGURES

The three Unpromising Hero fables of *The Prince and the Pauper* are unified in a remarkable number of ways. The most obvious of these is that all three are unmistakably instances of the one motif. A second unifying factor is an outgrowth of the first: all three heroes have double father-figures, and the fathers of each of the heroes are linked in some subtle way to those of the next, so as to forge a continuous chain. The bifurcation of the father-figure is most clearly represented in Tom Canty's case: John Canty, the thief who tyranizes his impoverished family, is the "ideal" father of a boy's Oedipal imagination—dirty, ugly, brutal, and swinishly ignorant. He is a man fit for the hanging King Edward finally promises him if Tom shall desire it. Tom's other father is as kindly as John Canty is odious. Father Andrew, "a good old priest whom the king had turned out of house and home with a pension of a few farthings," prepares the boy for his unsuspected royal vocation by teaching him to read Latin and to dream. Father Andrew, celibate, old, and nearly destitute, and consequently inconceivable as a rival, is another instance of perfect type casting.

Edward Tudor's father, Henry VIII, the Protestant king who has reduced Father Andrew to his pitiful circumstances, is in his own son's view not unlike John Canty. When the prince learns from the little pauper of John's cruelties, he comments, "Fathers be alike, mayhap. Mine hath not a doll's temper. He smiteth with a heavy hand, yet spareth me: he spareth me not with his tongue, though, sooth to say." Edward's feelings toward King Henry are, however, not entirely unfilial, as his genuine sorrow at the King's death demonstrates. But when Edward is booted out the palace gate in the pauper's rags, he inherits his double's father, John Canty, an entirely unambiguous figure. John's threatening presence follows him through much of his journey of initiation, but at every crisis he can turn to his kindly father-figure, Miles Hendon. The case of Adam in [Shakespeare's] *The Tale of Gamelyn* and *As You Like It* suggests that a servant makes an ideal kindly father-figure because he is by virtue of his social status a non-rival: and Miles is, in relation to his king, a servant.

Miles Hendon's dual paternity is especially interesting. His own kind father and the kind (and sickly) older brother who would have taken his father's place in the family are, although Miles has no knowledge of it, dead before the action commences. Miles's younger brother has become the head of his family and has married the woman Miles loves, a woman who also loves Miles. Hugh Hendon is as perfectly qualified in temperament and disposition to play the odious father-figure as John Canty is: he is "a tyrant who knows no pity." And what of Miles Hendon's kindly father-figure? Blake Andrews, a faithful old servant of the Hendon family, bears some resemblance to Gamelyn's Adam, but Blake's role is brief and shadowy: he is powerless to help Miles against the evil Hugh. (The coincidence of names, Blake Andrews and Father Andrew, is probably unintentional, but it underscores the similarity of the roles the two play.) Assistance finally comes to Miles from an unexpected quarter, from the deranged lad he has befriended. That lad is in actuality his king and as such stands *in loco parentis* [in place of a parent] to Miles, his most favored subject—his favorite "son." The evil brother Hugh flees from the presence of this boy-father to a deserved, albeit accidental, death.

Thus the novel effects the degradation of each hero's odious father-figure and provides for each an ideal kindly substitute: for Miles, a royal father who stands deeply in his debt; for Tom, an aged, celibate father; for Edward, a father who is at once his protector and his subject.

A UNIFIED NOVEL

In *The Adventures of Tom Sawyer* the hero and almost all his fellow villagers are engaged in frantic efforts to establish their artificial identities: the results are comic, sometimes amiably so, sometimes mordantly. In *The Prince and the Pauper* all three heroes are confronted with the deadly serious necessity of reestablishing their true identities. In a metaphoric sense, establishing his identity is always the business of the Unpromising Hero, but Mark Twain has made it the literal business of the heroes of this novel. The initial idea upon which the plot is based presupposes that Prince Edward and Tom Canty will suffer the denial of their identities, but the conception of Miles Hendon's problem did not dictate that it take this form. Yet consider what happens in Chapter XXV when Miles presents himself at Hendon Hall. The wicked Hugh, who has wrongfully possessed himself of the inheritance which belongs to Miles and has even taken possession of Miles's sweetheart, might well have been expected to try to murder the rightful claimant. Instead, he denies Miles's identity; he refuses to recognize him as his brother, and he forces all the people in his power, even the grief-stricken lady, to examine Miles, as if sympathetically and hopefully, and then to avow that they have never seen him before. In the denial of Miles Hendon's identity Mark Twain's craftsmanship is apparent: since collaborating on *The Gilded Age*, he had learned the art of fashioning a unified novel out of multiple plot strands by making those strands run parallel.

DREAM AS DOMINANT METAPHOR

The questioned identities of all three heroes receive added emphasis from the frequent references to dreams, and these references give a further pattern and unity to the whole work. Tom Canty's story begins with an account of the "empty grandeurs of his dreams"; on the night after the change of places has occurred, Edward lies down to sleep in Tom's straw, Tom on Edward's royal couch; in the middle of the night each boy wakes, thinks he is in his own bed and calls out that he has had a strange dream; but then the painful truth that it has not after all been a dream comes to each boy. The distinction between dream and reality is obscured for these two. Lady Edith, Miles Hendon's sweetheart, who has been compelled to become his brother's wife, tries to convince him that he too is living in a dream and although nothing can shake Miles's grip on the reality of his own situation, he fails to distinguish dream from actuality in the situation of the young king: he calls Edward "the Lord of the Kingdom of Dreams and Shadows" and after Edward has knighted him he calls himself "a Knight of the Kingdom of Dreams and Shadows."

A CHILDREN'S CLASSIC

I have cited only a representative selection of the elements Mark Twain employed to unify this triple-plotted novel—the dream as dominant metaphor, the quests for identity, the linking of sons through shared father-figures, the customary elements, in sum, of Unpromising Hero *Märchen*. The result is a book which hangs together exceptionally well: it is, and it deserves to be, a classic of children's literature. One can put it into the hands of a young reader confident that it will do more than hold his interest and provide moral instruction; it will also place before him in a simplified conceptual vocabulary a touchstone for testing the quality of novels. In characterization, in style, and in the articulation of structure and image and meaning, *The Prince and the Pauper is* exemplary among books accessible to younger children. One must, however, acknowledge that its conceptual vocabulary is so greatly simplified, its orientation so monotonously two-valued, that it comes short of the legitimate expectations of adult readers. I like to think that Mark Twain knew he had written a book exclusively for children and that his subtitle "A Tale for Young People of All Ages" was not a painfully accurate cliché, but a prediction, written with Horatian confidence, that he had produced a *monumentum aere perennius* [a timeless classic] scaled to the size of a child's world.

CHAPTER 3

Major Themes

Moralism Versus Determinism

Gladys Carmen Bellamy

In *Mark Twain as a Literary Artist* (1950), Gladys
Carmen Bellamy analyzes Twain's major works to
see what they reveal about his philosophy of life. She
concludes Twain had a major internal conflict between believing the individual was totally responsible for his or her actions and being convinced that
people had no influence whatsoever over the overwhelming dictates of the environment. According to
Bellamy, this conflict between Twain the rabid social
reformer and Twain the dogmatic determinist accounts for his difficulty in achieving unity in his
fiction, which is his chief failure as a literary artist.
Bellamy says this conflict is evident in *The Prince
and the Pauper* where Twain's zeal for humanitarian
reform was overcome by his pessimism, determinism, and preoccupation with the weaknesses of human nature.

Mark Twain's fiction is that part of his work in which, as
[critic] Bernard DeVoto noted, the artist stands most clearly
revealed, in his weakness and his strength. Two main forces
can be discerned, pulling against each other in [Twain's]
mind: on one hand, the idea of the ethical responsibility of the
individual man; on the other, an idea which transfers responsibility from the individual to the universal, thus releasing
man from all obligation for his own conduct. These two poles
of thought in his work have been variously observed. As early
as 1912, [his official biographer Albert Bigelow] Paine recognized this ideological conflict when he wrote that once ad-
mitting the postulate that existence

> is merely a sequence of cause and effect beginning with the
> primal atom . . . we have a theory that must stand or fall as a
> whole. We cannot say that man is a creature of circumstance

and then leave him free to select his circumstance, even in the minutest fractional degree.

And [Twain critic Edward] Wagenknecht wrote in 1935, "If Mark Twain is anything he is a moralist, yet there is no room for morality in his philosophy of life," while he spoke elsewhere of Mark Twain as "a fanatical determinist." Mr. Wagenknecht noticed that in one speech of the Connecticut Yankee the two poles of thought appear to exist simultaneously and that the "Gospel" itself contains an important passage that accords badly with Mark Twain's determinism: "Diligently train your ideas *upward* and still *upward* toward a summit where you will find your chiefest pleasure in conduct which, while contenting you, will . . . confer benefits upon your neighbor and the community." Or, as the laconic Puddn'head Wilson phrased it, "Let us endeavor so to live that when we come to die even the undertaker will be sorry." The conflict in Mark Twain's thought, then, has been recognized previously; but I know of no attempt, so far, to analyze the effect of that conflict upon his literary work.

Twain's Internal Conflict

That he himself recognized the conflict that went on inside him is clear. In 1898 he wrote to [his close friend and confidante Joseph] Twichell, concerning a prisoner held for assassinating the Empress of Austria:

> A man is either a free agent or he isn't. If a man is a free agent, this prisoner is responsible for what he has done; but if a man is not a free agent . . . there is no rational way of making this prisoner even partially responsible for it. . . . Logic is logic.

In 1904 he roundly scored his friend Twichell for his connection with party politics, because of its deteriorating effect upon "a man's mental and moral make-up." He pleaded with Twichell to "get out of that sewer" and then fumigate himself. But he added a postscript:

> I wish I could learn to remember that it is unjust and dishonorable to put blame upon the human race for any of its acts. For it did not make itself, it did not make its nature, it is merely a machine, it is moved wholly by outside influences, it has no hand in creating the outside influences nor in choosing which of them it will welcome or reject . . . ; wherefore, whatever the machine does . . . is the personal act of its Maker, and He, solely, is responsible. I wish I could learn to pity the human race instead of censuring it . . . and I could, if the outside influences of old habit were not so strong upon my machine.

His condemnations arose always from emotional attitudes, not from his reason. At another time he wrote to Twichell, "I know the human race's limitations, and this makes it my duty . . . to be fair to it." Still, he continued to rage. His letters, which he intended for publication, are overflowing with this rage. During the hard-fought Blaine-Cleveland campaign of 1884, he wrote to [writer and literary critic William Dean] Howells of those who think one way and vote another:

> *Isn't* human nature the most consummate sham and lie that was ever invented? Isn't man a creature to be ashamed of . . . ? Man, 'know thyself'—and then thou wilt despise thyself. . . . Hawley is howling for Blaine, Warner and Clark are eating their daily crow in the paper for him. . . . O Stultification, where is thy sting, O Slave, where is thy hickory!

In an 1892 article, "Concerning the Jews," he discussed race prejudices, adding: "I can stand any society. All that I care to know is that a man is a human being, that is enough for me; he can't be any worse." The following year he complained bitterly to Howells:

> I have been reading the morning paper . . . well knowing that I shall find in it the usual depravities and basenesses and hypocrisies and cruelties that make up civilization, and cause me to put in the rest of the day pleading for the damnation of the human race.

In 1905, he wrote to Twichell, who had been arguing the case for "progress," that neither the human heart nor the human brain had undergone any change since the beginning. But a little later . . . he wrote that the human brain *had* improved. The morals, alas, had not:

> . . . as inheritors of the mentality of our reptile ancestors we have improved the inheritance by a thousand grades; but in the matter of the morals which they left us we have gone backward as many grades. . . . Necessarily we started equipped with their perfect and blemishless morals; now . . . we have no real morals, but only artificial ones—morals created and preserved by the forced suppression of natural and hellish instincts. Yet we are dull enough to be vain of them.

> Certainly, we are a sufficiently comical invention, we humans. . . .

IDEOLOGICAL CONFLICT IN *THE PRINCE AND THE PAUPER*

The mind of Mark Twain was a workshop in which two creatures were constantly busy, a creature of hope and a creature of despair. Despite their enforced intimacy, they

MARK TWAIN ON DETERMINISM

In the following speech by The Boss in Mark Twain's A Connecticut Yankee in King Arthur's Court, *he says that all people's ideas are determined by forces outside themselves, and what is unique about a human being is but a minute fraction of the whole person.*

Training—training is everything; training is all there is *to* a person. We speak of nature; . . . what we call by that misleading name is merely heredity and training. We have no thoughts of our own . . . they are transmitted to us, trained into us. All that is original in us . . . can be covered up . . . by the point of a cambric needle, all the rest being . . . inherited from . . . the Adam-clan of grasshopper or monkey from whom our race has been so . . . unprofitably developed. And as for me, all that I think about in this pathetic drift between the eternities is to . . . save that one microscopic atom in me that is truly *me:* the rest may land in Sheol for all I care.

Mark Twain, *A Connecticut Yankee in King Arthur's Court,* 1889.

were not on good terms; their natures were far too different. Sometimes one would cow the other into temporary submission so that he could finish a piece of work—hurriedly, perhaps; but often one—that is, whichever began first— would be challenged by the other, who would insist on doing a part of the job his way. There were always two Mark Twains, the Moralist *versus* the Determinist. [In his short story] *The Man That Corrupted Hadleyburg,* [a] . . . clash between moralism and determinism is discerned more readily than in the longer fiction, since the narrow scope brings the opposing ideas into closer juxtaposition. But the ideological conflict that is basic in the Hadleyburg tale appears again and again. It appears briefly even in *The Prince and the Pauper,* which grew out of his reading *The Prince and the Page,* by Charlotte M. Yonge. In the Yonge story a nobleman lives for years disguised as a blind beggar. Mark Twain decided that he would not only disguise a prince as a beggar, but also a beggar as a prince. He chose Edward VI, small son of Henry VIII, as his subject and began to study the period from books and maps. He wrote about half of the story in 1877 and completed it in 1880.

So far as structure is concerned, this book is perhaps his finest achievement. He wrote to Howells, "It begins at 9 A.M.,

Jan. 27, 1547 . . . and goes on for three weeks—till the . . . coronation grandeurs in Westminster Abbey, Feb. 20." The narrow compass and the contrast formula both laid restraints upon him; add the fact that the period of the action was far enough away to allow him aesthetic distance and the further fact that the chief characters are boys, and the extraordinary unity which he achieved in *The Prince and the Pauper* stands explained. In a recent article, [Twain critic] A.L. Vogelback notes that it was the first work on which critics mainly agreed that Mark Twain displayed "notable abilities as a serious writer and literary artist." For *The Prince and the Pauper* complied with literary conventions of the time, while *Tom Sawyer* and later *Huckleberry Finn*, lying outside the tradition of correctness and imitation, puzzled and disturbed the critics.

TWAIN AS PESSIMISTIC DETERMINIST

This book was Mark Twain's first full-length study of the power of determining environment and circumstance. The transformation of beggar into prince and vice versa was effected by a mere change of clothes. The significance of clothes in the work of Mark Twain rests upon some such explanation as this: since the world judges by outward appearance, the clothes one wears become a part of the exterior determining circumstances which decide what everyone will be. His original intention had been to center attention upon the real prince, accounting for the "mildness which distinguished Edward VI's reign from those that preceded and followed it" by having him experience at first hand the hardships of his subjects. But, as the story progressed, Mark Twain gave most of his attention to the pressure of environment upon the moral fiber of the small bogus prince, Tom Canty of Offal Court. Even the humanitarian's zeal for reform could not overcome the pessimistic determinist's interest in the weaknesses of human nature. Tom lapses from a sturdy rebellion in which he denounces servants for troubling him "with offices that harass the spirit and shame the soul, they misbecoming any but a doll, that hath nor brains nor hands to help itself withal," into a slothful enjoyment of the splendors that surround him. Finally he sinks into a corrupt resignation in which, when his mother recognizes him in one of his public appearances, he says, "I do not know you, woman!" Here the conflict between moralism and determinism appears: Tom, brought to this shameful state by circumstances beyond his control, was assailed so strongly by his conscience that his shame "withered his stolen royalty. His grandeurs were stricken valueless; they seemed to fall away from him like rotten rags."

This incident occurred upon the very day that restoration was made to the rightful prince. One wonders what would have happened to Tom Canty if his masquerade had been prolonged. Mark Twain realized the importance of both environment and heredity, but *The Prince and the Pauper* shows environment as the stronger force. If heredity had triumphed, the real prince might have returned to his palace unchanged. This tale of rags and robes uncovers Mark Twain's characteristic thought-patterns. Although he had planned the story to show the broadening and mellowing of the prince, his chief emphasis falls upon the deterioration which has begun in the other boy. Human nature's frailty always engrossed him. . . .

TWAIN'S ACHILLES HEELS

As a moralist, [Mark Twain] raged at men because they are what they are; as a determinist, he raged at the primary forces or environing circumstances that make men what they are. . . . He had, in fact, two Achilles heels where his art was concerned—pity and rage, rage and pity—and he was always torn between the two moods. He carried within his soul the intolerable burden of pity, and frequently his rage was only a mechanism set up in self-defense.

The German critic Friedrich Schönemann finds in the temperament of Mark Twain an example of the theory of romantic irony. It is true enough that he had the age-old conflict of head-and-heart; yet his particular conflict seems to have reversed what we ordinarily mean by those terms. For it was in his emotions, his keen conscience, that he most severely condemned mankind, while in calmer moods his intellect and his reason tended to sway him away from such narrow and bitter thinking. But the spirit of his stern and uncompromising conscience generally triumphed; and mankind remained for him to the end only "the damned human race."

Twain's Views on Human Nature

Robert A. Wiggins

In the following excerpt from *Mark Twain: Jackleg Novelist* (1964) Robert A. Wiggins says the flaws in *The Prince and the Pauper* arise from Twain's propaganda purpose in writing the novel, the implausible sequence of events and characters, and Twain's failure to effectively transplant some of his beliefs to a foreign setting and alien culture. According to Wiggins, Twain's hatred of the monarchy motivated his writing of the novel and inspired the development of the theme of mercy. He says the work is principally directed at the young and naive mind and suggests that goodness and generosity are qualities inherent in human nature.

To some extent Twain departs from his principles of realism in *A Connecticut Yankee*, and in its closely related predecessor *The Prince and the Pauper*, chiefly as a consequence of the propaganda purpose of these novels. Both books are too weighted with sociocritical ideas to be entirely satisfying as novels. *Huckleberry Finn* was critical of the society it portrayed, but in that instance the ideas seem to have grown logically out of the material examined, whereas *The Prince and the Pauper* and *A Connecticut Yankee* give the impression that the material was selected to illustrate a thesis.

UNIFIED PURPOSE AND PLOT

The writer, of course, approaches the composition of any work with a body of beliefs which he holds, but the process of writing is also one of discovery. It is now generally a critical commonplace to observe that, as he writes, the novelist gradually learns what his story is, and not until it is quite complete does he really discover his story. Moreover, this discovery does not necessarily suggest the author's complete awareness. *Huckleberry Finn* seems to have been composed somewhat after this fashion, but in the writing of *The Prince and the Pauper* and *A Connecticut Yankee,* Twain thought he knew in advance what he wanted his stories to be. They do not unfold themselves to the reader as does *Huckleberry Finn,* but rather marshall themselves as evidence to prove a point. But this is not to say that they are logically and coherently organized about a central issue, for in organization they are typical of Twain's discursive approach. However, a rough unity of purpose is discernible within them that does accord them some measure of design beyond Twain's customary achievement.

The Prince and the Pauper was published in December, 1881, before *Huckleberry Finn,* because, although the latter was begun almost immediately after the publication of *Tom Sawyer* in 1876, Twain's "tank ran dry," and *Huckleberry Finn* was shelved for several years before Twain returned to it and completed the book in 1883. *The Prince and the Pauper* was begun in the summer of 1877; it too was shelved for a time, but was taken up with *Huckleberry Finn* again in 1880, and then Twain alternately worked on them both, completing *The Prince and the Pauper* first.

Twain outlined the plot with more care than was his custom in order to keep the story within the limits of historical fact and to illustrate his thesis. Because he was forced to stay within the historical time between the death of Henry VIII and the prince's coronation, he could not take the discursive liberties of *Tom Sawyer* and *Huckleberry Finn;* moreover, his thesis controlled the kind of events he could select or invent as relevant to his purpose. As a consequence he produced a plot unified in the conventional sense understood by the novel-reading audience of his time.

The plot hinges upon a variation of the twin theme—a constantly recurring motif for Twain. Two look-alikes trade places. One is Tom Canty, a slum-dwelling boy raised in a blighted area of London; the other is the young prince, later to become Edward VI. The story alternates between Tom's uneasy masquerade as a young monarch almost to the moment of his coronation and the picaresque adventure of the young king. The latter plot gets the greater emphasis. In company with a dispossessed nobleman as his protector, the king is subjected to a series of episodes in which he is regarded as mentally deranged. During this revealing experience, the prince learns a great deal about his subjects and their sufferings under oppressive laws and economic exploitation.

The book was acclaimed as a newer and higher achievement than any of his previous fiction. Certainly his earlier misgivings about its reception were dispelled. He had told [his friend and confidante] Mrs. A.W. Fairbanks that it would appear without his name, "such grave and stately work being considered by the world to be above my proper level." His wife and [writer and critic William Dean] Howells both assured him that it should appear as his own work; indeed, Olivia was more enthusiastic about this book than any other Twain had produced. Her critical judgment would seem to have been vindicated by the success of *The Prince and the Pauper,* but it should not be surprising. Her tastes reflected her upbringing, and they were those of conventionally accepted standards of the day. *The Prince and the Pauper* more than any of Twain's earlier works met those standards and consequently was judged more successful, meeting with greater critical and popular favor than either *Tom Sawyer* or *Huckleberry Finn,* though it did not match the commercial success of his earlier books.

CONTEMPT FOR THE MONARCHY

To Howells in March, 1880, Twain described what he felt to be the controlling purpose of his tale in *The Prince and the Pauper:*

> My idea is to afford a realizing sense of the exceeding severity of the laws of the day by inflicting some of their penalties upon the king himself and allowing him a chance to see the rest of them applied to others—all of which is to account for certain mildnesses which distinguished Edward VI's reign from those that preceded and followed it.

Twain took the text for his exemplum from *The Merchant of Venice* and quotes it in the introduction:

> The quality of mercy . . .
> > is twice bless'd;
> It blesseth him that gives, and him that takes;
> 'Tis mightiest in the mightiest: it becomes
> The throned monarch better than his crown.

The text is kept constantly before the reader up to the closing words of the tale:

> "What dost thou know of suffering and oppression? I and my people know, but not thou."

The reign of Edward VI was a singularly merciful one for

those harsh times. Now that we are taking leave of him let us
try to keep this in our minds, to his credit.

The theme is based upon the assumption of moral progress
and enlightenment since the time of Edward VI. It was a
view of progress that he later abandoned, maintaining that
man had made progress in materialities only. But in *The
Prince and the Pauper* Twain asserts by way of a general epi-
logue that mankind had made some moral progress. The assertion, however, is only incidental to his favorable contrast
of the United States to another country still led by a king. No
book by Twain fails in some way to reflect his hatred of
monarchy, even an enlightened monarchy, and *The Prince
and the Pauper* is no exception. The statement reflects
Twain's motive in developing his theme of mercy and also
indicates the theme that was to receive a fuller treatment in
A Connecticut Yankee:

> One hears about the "hideous Blue-Laws of Connecticut,"
> and is accustomed to shudder piously when they are men-
> tioned . . . There has never been a time—under the Blue-Laws
> or any other—when above FOURTEEN crimes were punishable
> by death in Connecticut. But in England, within the memory
> of men who are still hale in body and mind, TWO HUNDRED

TWAIN ON DEMOCRACY

*Even when he felt American democracy was failing,
Twain—as this excerpt shows—still was passionate about
the equality of all men.*

The American dogma, rightly translated, makes this assertion:
that every man is of right born free, that is, without master or
owner; and also that every man is of right born his neighbor's
political equal—that is, possessed of every legal right and
privilege which his neighbor enjoys and not debarred from
aspiring to any dignity to which his neighbor may attain.
When a man accepts this rendering of that gospel, it is the
same as proclaiming that he believes that whoever is born
and lives in a country where he is denied a privilege accorded
his neighbor—even though his neighbor be a king—is not a
freeman; that when he consents to wear the stigma described
by the word "subject," he has merely consented to call himself
a slave by a gentler epithet; and that where a king is there is
but one person in that nation who is not a slave.

Quoted in Philip S. Foner, *Mark Twain: Social Critic.* New York: International
Publishers, 1966.

AND TWENTY-THREE crimes were punishable by death! These facts are worth knowing—and worth thinking about, too.

UNREALISTIC EVENTS AND CHARACTERS

The book is an historical romance, "Tale for Young People of All Ages," as the subtitle proclaims, and not a bad one. Indeed, in its day it was a positive advance over the usual fare offered to a juvenile audience. Twain was essentially a realist, and even a romance, he believed, should be told with realistic details. He contrasts the world of the court with that of the common people and does not stay his hand from painting the filth, poverty, drunkenness, and brutality of the people laboring under cruel and unjust laws. Twain portrayed the conditions as faithfully as his limited knowledge, gained from reading a few sources, would permit.

But even if one accepts the fantastic exchange of identity between the prince and the pauper that begins the tale, the following events cannot be said to proceed realistically. The numerous adventures involving the prince in his picaresque wanderings are no more unusual in their own cultural and historical setting than Huck Finn's in another time and place, but there is a vast difference between the two in the elementary forms of their treatment. Verisimilar [factually based] details are supplied, but Twain does not really seem to desire the reader to feel any sense of immediacy in the events. In *Huckleberry Finn*, the reader feels himself to be present as events unfold before him, but in *The Prince and the Pauper* Twain reminds the reader that the events after all took place long ago; this is a legend that he is narrating for an audience: "It may be that the wise and the learned believed it in the old days; it may be that only the unlearned and the simple loved it and credited it." The reader is frequently reminded that he should not even pretend to be present.

Let us skip a number of years.

London was fifteen hundred years old, and was a great town—for that day. . . .

Let us privileged ones hurry to the great banqueting room and have a glance at matters there while Tom is being made ready for the imposing occasion. . . .

And so we leave them. . . .

Let us go backwards a few hours. . . .

Let us change the tense for convenience. . . .

Twain repeatedly addresses the reader directly and reminds him that he is outside them. The method does not follow the principle of making the events "seem reality." The numerous footnotes citing authorities for the actuality of the events portrayed cannot make them "seem reality"; indeed, in attempting to convince the reader of their truth, they only remind him more that the tale is fiction and not a chronicle of actuality.

Twain does not demonstrate any historical sense on a significant level. He asserts, for example, the naive notion that the common man reacts universally and fundamentally the same. Tom Canty, so far as Twain understood, in another time and place was a Tom Sawyer whose romantic dreams came true, but he had no conception that the difference in circumstances could also account for the differences in their characters. The assumption that the only difference between the prince and the pauper was in their clothing is manifestly absurd. Even if their raiment is symbolic, the proposition is untenable, but Twain persists in working it out to an improbable solution.

BENEVOLENT VIEW OF HUMAN NATURE

The Prince and the Pauper certainly is not a realistic view of mankind, or boyhood, distilled in the pages of pseudo-history. It may be regarded as a kind of legend and as such embodies an ideal that mankind should serve; but inevitably, in the light of his nature, man must fall short of achieving. The story is then directed to the mythic, primitive, juvenile mind, and to this mind it speaks a message: mankind is fundamentally good, and the virtues of charity, mercy, and magnanimity are inherent in man's nature. It is the message of *Huckleberry Finn* in another range of material. The two books, which he often worked on simultaneously, afford a striking contrast: although the beliefs about the nature of mankind informing both books are similar, *Huckleberry Finn* is more convincing because the body of belief is associated with the folk from which it sprang, while in *The Prince and the Pauper* it is forced upon an alien culture.

A Democratic Fable

James Cox

In the following excerpt from *Mark Twain: The Fate of Humor* (1966) James Cox claims that explanations by Twain critics for the failure of *The Prince and the Pauper* are partial and inadequate. He says at the core of the failure of the novel is its lack of humor. While the book is an interesting democratic fable, Cox says that character development is sacrificed to plot and that Twain's attempt to be serious showed an insecurity in the author as to his own identity. The novel is a betrayal of Twain's true genius.

Though the failure of *The Prince and the Pauper* . . . is universally acknowledged, explanations for it are diverse and often conflicting. One of the most common accounts of the book's deficiency is that Mark Twain, off his home ground, did not really know English life as he knew life on the Mississippi. Unable to assimilate the texture of the alien history into his book, he surrendered the marvelous realism of Tom Sawyer to the strained sentiment of *The Prince and the Pauper*. Another argument is that Mark Twain attempted simply to meet the juvenile audience and thus produced nothing more than a conventional juvenile book. There is also the explanation that Mark Twain, surrendering to the canons of genteel taste, wrote for his wife's approval, which is to say that he consciously pursued the saccharine sentimentality on which she presumably battened.

All of these explanations are partially true. Not only do they shed light on the book; they can all be corroborated by evidence from the life and letters of Mark Twain. Certainly Mark Twain did not have the easy aplomb in the English scene he determined to portray that he had along the Mississippi of his memory. For in moving from St. Petersburg to sixteenth-century London, he was moving from his personal past to the *literary* past. In the one fiction he was recon structing experience; in the other he was fabricating a tale. And certainly he was writing consciously for the juvenile audience. The dedication of the book "To those good-mannered and agreeable children, Susy and Clara Clemens" has an irony, which whether it is intentional or unintentional, measures him and gives credence to the argument that he was writing for approval.

Yet *The Prince and the Pauper* is clearly addressed to an adult audience as much as or more than *Tom Sawyer* was. It is ostensibly more satirical than its predecessor. Certainly for anyone interested in Mark Twain's thought or social criticism, *The Prince and the Pauper* is a far more valuable repository than *Tom Sawyer*. His democratic impulses and broadly liberal humanitarianism are evident here in a way they had never been in his earlier work. Still the book fails—and fails decisively. It is actually an extremely weak performance, interesting only in the light it can throw upon the success which preceded it and the masterpiece soon to follow.

TWAIN'S EFFORTS TO OUTDO *TOM SAWYER*

His failure lay, in part, in his attempt to repeat the triumph of *Tom Sawyer,* an almost inevitable impulse after the success of the earlier book. Mark Twain was in much the same position he had occupied after his first travel book. He had carved out a great success for himself and the invitation to keep at the same line was strong. His career after *Tom Sawyer* shows much the same confused groping and futility so prominent after *The Innocents Abroad*. First, he began *Huckleberry Finn,* wrote for a time with a good deal of intensity, but, unable to push the book beyond its sustained opening movement, he gave up, shelving what was to be his greatest discovery in order to try possibilities he had already realized. After collaborating with [author and playwright] Bret Harte on the drama *Ah, Sin,* he involved himself in a drama of his own in which the "garrulous, good natured old Simon Wheeler" would be forced back into service in the role of detective. When that project proved a disaster, he began work on *The Prince and the Pauper.* He had intended to write a drama—the dramatic element in *Tom Sawyer* apparently was playing itself out in these groping theatrical efforts—but wrote a story instead. Before he was to complete *The Prince and the Pauper,* he involved himself in the Whittier birthday fiasco [where he unintentionally gave insult to the literary establishment]; took a two-year European travel jaunt; returned to America, where in November,1879, he accomplished the marvelous success of the Grant speech which he felt atoned in part for the galling Whittier birthday failure; and finally completed *A Tramp Abroad,* surely the dreariest of all his travel books. During his difficulties with *A Tramp Abroad,* he again resumed work on *The Prince and the Pauper* and completed it at Quarry Farm during the summer of 1880, while he was also back at work on *Huckleberry Finn*—if Walter Blair is right in his excellent surmises on the subject.

Yet the failure of *The Prince and the Pauper* is as much a result of Mark Twain's attempt to surpass *Tom Sawyer* as to repeat his old success. Quite clearly he meant to show himself not simply a humorous and commercial artist. He wrote to [author and critic William Dean] Howells that he did not care whether it sold or not, so much had he enjoyed inventing it—implying that the book was to be an elegant show piece more for art than money. Above all, it was not to be merely funny.

THE NOVEL LACKS HUMOR

Here was the heart of its failure. It lacked humor. It is tiresome because it strives to be serious rather than humorous. Now, of course, this begs the question of the nature of humor, but the discussion of *Tom Sawyer* goes far toward answering that question. In that book, Mark Twain's humor had lain precisely in the discovery of a character who could create the world as play. In this book, however, he sacrifices his character to a plot designed to illustrate the injustices of monarchy. To be sure, the book is in certain ways an interesting democratic fable, turning on a plot device which elevates a commoner to a king and reduces a king to a commoner. But the characters are sacrificed to the device of the plot; the book is a fable more than a fiction, which is to say that it subordinates action to a set of assumed values. Though the values may be admirable, the result is essentially static and impotent. For the more Samuel Clemens attempts to be "serious" the more he betrays his genius, Mark Twain. Rather than being repressed by Mark Twain, as [suggested by critic Van Wyck] Brooks . . . Clemens was suppressing Mark Twain. It was this "seriousness" which Howells ceremoniously approved in his unsigned review in the New York *Tribune* (25 October 1881). "The fascination of the narrative and the strength of the implied moral are felt at once," observed Howells, "and increase together to the end in a degree which will surprise those who have found nothing but drollery in Mark Twain's books, and have not perceived the artistic sense and the strain of deep earnestness underlying his humor."

CRITICS DEVALUE HUMOR

Howells' remarks offer a way into the heart of the "problem" of Mark Twain. The modern reader, possessing a perspective on the Gilded Age, would classify the remarks as simply one more example of the genteel aesthetic. But to patronize Howells' taste on such a basis usually eventuates in covertly substituting a new genteel tradition for the old. Thus people who freely condemn Howells' judgment on *The Prince and the Pauper* believe no more than he in Mark Twain's humor. They too, it often develops, want Mark Twain to be serious; the only difference is that their focus upon Mark Twain has the inevitable advantage which a perspective of eighty years provides. Their taste is no better than Howells', really, and their aesthetic is practically the same. Thus their reasons for not liking *The Prince and the Pauper* do not revolve around the fact that it lacks humor, but that it is not realistic; or that it is a commercial exploit; or that Mark Twain's knowledge of history was cursory; or that his theory of history and his idea of progress were inadequate; or that Mark Twain "sold out" to the genteel and juvenile markets. There is evidence to support all these contentions, but none is definitive. All remain partial answers.

THE NOVEL AS DEMOCRATIC FABLE

Their very partiality brings us back to the central failure of the book—its apparent commitment to humor, yet its failure to be humorous. Not that Samuel Clemens had to write humorous works; he did not have to, but Mark Twain did, and in this book Samuel Clemens clearly could not surrender to the idea of being a humorist. He wished to exploit his humorous genius without fully committing himself to humor. That is why he considered concealing his authorship, but at the last moment, after Howells expressed delight in the book, he decided to go on intrepidly and reveal himself. His indecision—it could have been mock-indecision—is an index to his uncertainty about his own identity in the book.

This uncertainty manifests itself within the book as a failure to believe in humor. Thus, "Mark Twain," the genius of Samuel Clemens' humor, is betrayed in the name of piety and "noble" sentiment.

The sign of the betrayal lies in the way in which the characters are subordinated to the plot. The plot, which hinges on the device of mistaken identity, rides the action, seeming always to be imposed from without. It presents coincidence in the guise of trick, not of fate; and its logic, instead of evoking that sense of inevitability which relates character to event, is a mechanism which processes the characters and times the action. In many ways, the plot—with its devices, tricks, and surface exposure—is a comic plot, and it would be wrong to deplore its lack of tragic doom. But the plot is not finally humorous, for it is designed to point a moral. More than being a juvenile romance, an adventure story, or a comedy, the book is a fable—a democratic fable. That fable, which few critics of Mark Twain have elucidated, discloses through the device of mistaken identities, how the "divine right" of monarchy comes from the capacity of the commoner to *remember* the action in his remote past by means of which the king transferred the power to him. Seen as a democratic fable, the book is remarkably worked out, the plot acting as an analogue of the "moral" or "truth" toward which the action points. Thus the prince and the pauper, once the trick of their change is effected, cannot prove who they are. King and commoner are finally one; they are divided only to serve the purposes of "fiction," something which, as Mark Twain observed in his preface, *could* have happened. Only through Tom Canty's memory is the true king proved to be king instead of pretender.

CLEMENS BETRAYS TWAIN

Yet the book remains a fable and not a humorous narrative of boyhood adventure. This in itself is not bad; there are worse things than fables. But—and here the difficulty comes in—the book is Mark Twain too. In a sense he was right to sign his name, for there is enough of his characteristic style present to establish his identity beyond doubt. But it is Mark Twain betrayed. For insofar as Mark Twain *is* present, the impulse necessarily is toward humor—which is to say the impulse is to discover the world as entertainment. But since Mark Twain's humor is imprisoned in the plot, it is subverted; in effect, it is being used for a "serious purpose." This is why the book seems so sentimental. Lacking the courage of its deepest impulse, it betrays that impulse and forces humor to serve a noble purpose instead of forcing all noble purposes to serve humor.

The Prince and the Pauper was not Mark Twain's first failure; in many of the early sketches he had done no more than exercise clichés or indulge in reflexive repetitions of successful "acts." And after *The Innocents Abroad,* there had been a long moment in which he had done no more than prostitute his talent in a series of futile gestures, as if he were a literary entrepreneur who could buy experience by hiring reporters to have his experiences for him. But all these failures represented baldly commercial ventures—attempts to capitalize his humor. *The Prince and the Pauper,* however, was a failure of an entirely different order. Instead of trying to "sell" his genius, Samuel Clemens was betraying it. He was submitting to the other invitation which lures the humorist—the invitation to be "serious"; it would be an invitation which would come again and again, and it was perhaps more subtle and dangerous than the commercialism which was equally difficult to resist. For if in commercializing himself, Samuel Clemens was wasting his genius, in trying to be serious he was failing to believe in it.

Twain's Ambivalent Political Stance

Louis J. Budd

In *Mark Twain: Social Philosopher*, Louis J. Budd
says Mark Twain was deeply concerned with the
political questions of his day and was an amateur
statesman in his own right. He shows how much of
Twain's fiction reflected specific topical issues. In
the following excerpt he links *The Prince and the
Pauper* with the debate over the severity of Connecticut Blue Laws in which British commentators at-
tacked the political and religious tyranny of the
founding Puritans, claiming government by the
people was more oppressive than by a hereditary
ruling class. Budd concludes, however, that on close
examination, the novel presents a mixed message:
Although democratic values are touted, royalty is
treated respectfully and the characters revere their
rulers. Budd cautions against making generaliza-
tions as to inconsistencies in Mark Twain's political
views, saying they need to be assessed as they developed over the years in response to the events of his
times and attitudes of his peers.

The Prince and the Pauper (1882) seems doomed to a mar-
ginal life outside the cluster of Twain's enduring books and
yet apart from the ones that will inevitably be forgotten; no
responsible critic has praised or condemned all of it. Only
his third novel, it is much less mixed in performance, however, than in purpose. Though Twain's recurring fascination
with the horrors of losing personal or social identity and his
release in using the uncomplicated child as spokesman
pumped energy into its veins, it has many desiccating
patches of stock sentiment and plotting as a beggar and a
king accidentally switch places. These weaknesses have

Excerpted from *Mark Twain: Social Philosopher*, by Louis J. Budd. Copyright © 1962
by Indiana University Press. Reprinted with permission from the author.

been blamed on his Nook Farm friends, who urged him to avoid rowdy humor and generally elevate his tone. But *The Prince and the Pauper* also owes some of its strength to their belief that worth-while literature often bears on public questions. Whatever its private sources, it drew vitally on an argument interesting to loyal residents of Connecticut.

CONNECTICUT LAWS ATTACKED

As part of the continuing duel of scolding across the Atlantic, a writer for *Blackwood's Edinburgh Magazine* of April, 1870 had cited the political and religious despotism set up by the New World Puritans and had made their Blue Laws his detailed example in contending that majorities are more tyrannical than a hereditary ruling class. Spokesmen for New England were quick to answer that *Blackwood's*, because of its own religious and political bias, sneered habitually at the American tradition. When interest kept growing, Samuel Peters' trouble-making book was reprinted in 1876, the same year *The True-Blue Laws of Connecticut and New Haven* was published by J. Hammond Trumbull—private donor of the cryptic epigraphs for *The Gilded Age*. Twain at once read this scholarly answer to Peters' myth-ridden indictment of our colonial ancestors; in fact he bought and marked up two copies, as he sometimes did with books he used both in [his two places of residency] Hartford and Elmira. Trumbull alerted him to the debate if he had not followed it before and also chalked out the best rebuttal— an exposé of the severity underlying British criminal law. Within a few months Twain considered himself to be working on *The Prince and the Pauper*.

He first thought of setting it in modern England. A few years earlier he had been moved by seeing a British judge give fourteen years at hard labor to a "humbly clad young woman" whose husband had forced her into a petty crime. But, sensing sticky problems with the plot and British dignity, he soon dropped the notion of building his story around the living Prince of Wales; well read in history, he easily found an opening in the sixteenth century to highlight British practices that existed near the same time as the notorious Blue Laws and were much harsher. Fittingly, taking a closer look had a softening effect on Twain as well as on his royal hero, and he tersely jotted in his notebook for 1879, "I disfavor capital punishment." Though he still grumbled elsewhere about the opposite fault of being too merciful, he could now in better conscience act shocked because, even up into his own century, British law had carried a death sentence for two hundred and twenty-three crimes.

To pound in his point Twain even went on beyond the end of his plot to a "General Note" declaring that the maligned laws of Connecticut "were about the first SWEEPING DEPARTURE FROM JUDICIAL ATROCITY which the 'civilized' world had seen." For the reader who needed any further prompting, [critic and author William Dean] Howells' review emphasized that Twain had exposed the "stupid cruelty" of "those horrible good old times" in England. However, the debunking and its immediate purpose were clear to anybody who looked beneath the comedy and melodrama buoying up the grim passages. According to [Republican politician and U.S. President] Rutherford Hayes—who was a more curious mixture of Liberal and conservative ideas than Twain himself—his older children understood *The Prince and the Pauper* as the "only defense, or explanation rather, of the Puritan codes of our New England ancestor," and a British critic growled that it meant to convict his country of a still lingering "barbarism" and "so, by contrast, whitewash this embarrassing Blue business."

TWAIN AGAINST INTOLERANCE

The British critic also growled at a "general Protestant tone." Twain might have answered that he had pulled most of his punch on religious matters, as *A Connecticut Yankee* would show by comparison. It is true that only luck stopped an insane Holy Hermit from murdering the young king, but ragged Tom Canty was helped and educated by a "good old priest." Rather than lighting up the past crimes of Rome when he showed some Baptists being burned for heresy, Twain was commenting on the rigors of intolerance. In 1881 he felt impelled to undercut a genial talk about our Puritan fathers by recalling their harshness toward the Quakers and their passion for "liberty to worship as they required us to worship." Spurred on by [U.S. lawyer and orator] Robert G. Ingersoll's agnostic essays, he was becoming hostile to formal religion, Protestant as well as Catholic.

MIXED PURPOSE ON THE NOVEL

The strongest British complaint was that *The Prince and the Pauper* created a "misty atmosphere of Scott's chivalry in

which floats all the flunkeyism, aristocratic oppression, and
so forth, of all or any later period, as revealed to Columbia's
stern eye." In other words, Twain had taken the stance of a
New World republican more firmly than ever before, and
hindsight shows that he had started to warm up for *A Connecticut Yankee. The Prince and the Pauper* was still many
degrees cooler, however, than Hank Morgan's insults or the
hot asides in *Huckleberry Finn.* Though it often patronized
its characters from the heights of a superior present, almost
as many other touches were wistful over the chivalric past;
though its haughty prince was often laughable, he matured
into an admirable king. In denouncing it as a "libel on the
English Court" the British *Academy* went much too far. Its
only vigorous passages of satire pounced on the bevy of
high-ranking assistants at the King's dressing and dinner ta-
bles, a pet Yankee peeve that Twain had voiced against the
Hawaiian court in 1866. In 1882 these passages must have
sounded like a provocative echo of the Radicals' groans
about the expensive court circle supported in the budget for
Buckingham Palace and must have speeded up if not caused
the drop in the British market for Twain's books that started
around this time.

However, the basic idea of royalty is usually treated with
respect throughout the entire novel, whose closing emphasis falls on the fact that the reign of Edward VI was a "singularly merciful one." His coldness before his own troubles
begin seems mostly meant for proving that humanity grows
out of experience teaching you to imagine yourself in the
sufferer's place—a point central to W.E.H. Lecky's *History of
European Morals,* which Twain reread several times. After
his early blunders the sturdy little prince rises to a mercy
and heroism that justify the loyalty of stalwart Miles Hendon, who humbly accepts his share of the royal largess scat-
tered to help a happy ending; this well-born pair is many
firm mental and moral cuts above the "delighted and noisy
swarm of human vermin" making up the common people.
Furthermore, within its solid pity for the poor *The Prince
and the Pauper* draws a sharp line between the docile paupers and "tramps and ruffians," the fake beggars or thieving
vagrants whose march across the countryside borrows from
Twain's fretting about the drifters spawned by the American
depression of 1873. Tom Canty and his father neatly typify
this ambivalence toward the submerged masses, who are, in

any event, loyal to the crown with Twain's blessing. Perhaps such undemocratic reverence was overridden for genteel readers when Tom—because he otherwise had to deny knowing his mother—cooperated in proving the identity of the true king, but his cheerful abdication also smacks of the theme that uneasy lies the head burdened with the crown's duties. The juvenile audience that continues to enjoy Twain's tale surely sees it in terms of high-minded, care-worn kings and their faithful subjects.

The Need for Educated, Compassionate Rulers

Howard G. Baetzhold

In *Mark Twain and John Bull,* Howard G. Baetzhold
considers the role played by British writers in shaping the social, political, and philosophical ideas of
Mark Twain. In the following excerpt, Baetzhold describes the influence of British historian W.E. Lecky
on Twain's views on human nature. Baetzhold says
Lecky's influence in *The Prince and the Pauper* is
clear given the primary emphasis of the novel on Edward's education, the role of conscience in the actions of Tom Canty, and the description of the impact
of superstitious beliefs on human affairs. He concludes the novel was not anti-British or against the
monarchy, nor was it thematically concerned with
democracy or egalitarianism. Rather the main theme
was the central influence of education on developing
compassion, through "realizing" or directly experiencing the suffering of fellow human beings.

When Clemens announced to [his friend and literary critic
William Dean] Howells that he hoped "to afford a realizing
sense" of the harshness of life in Tudor times by exposing
Edward directly to some of the unjust laws, he was echoing
a concept derived from . . . British author William Edward
Hartpole Lecky. From his first encounter with Lecky's *History of European Morals from Augustus to Charlemagne*
(probably during the summer of 1874), he had read, marked,
and inwardly digested many of its arguments. Often he
noted marginally his agreement or disagreement with what
the historian said, or even with how he said it. But at one
point, after revising several clumsy constructions in the text,
he revealed an abiding affection: "It is so noble a book, & so
beautiful a book, that I don't wish it to have even trivial

faults in it." And he would continue to borrow ideas and incidents from it for the remainder of his writing career. . . .

In *The Prince and the Pauper* Lecky's influence seems three-fold, stemming from the historian's examination of the conflicting moral theories of the "intuitionists" and the "utilitarians"; his emphasis on education as a stimulus to the imagination; and his portrait of man's subjection to fear and superstition down through the ages.

The first two of these elements appear in the historian's long opening chapter. Because they were to be important to Clemens' future works, as well as to *The Prince and the Pauper*, they deserve discussion in some detail.

THE INTUITIVE VERSUS UTILITARIAN DEBATE

For many years to come Clemens would implicitly carry on what [Twain critic] Walter Blair has called his "discussion with Lecky" concerning the relative value of the two systems of moral theory characterized by the historian as "the stoical, the intuitive, the independent or the sentimental" and "the epicurean, the inductive, the utilitarian, or the selfish." The "intuitive" view, which Lecky espoused, argues that moral choices are governed by an innate moral sense, a "power of perceiving" that some qualities (like benevolence, chastity, or veracity) are better than others. A natural accompaniment to this power is a sense of *duty*, an obligation to cultivate the good qualities and suppress their opposites. This sense, in turn, becomes "in itself, and apart from all consequences," a sufficient reason for following any particular course of action. The "utilitarian" theory, to which Clemens was increasingly drawn over the years, *denies* that man possesses any such innate perception of virtue. Rather, his standards of right and wrong, his consideration of the "comparative excellence of . . . feelings and actions," depend solely on the degree to which those feelings and actions are conducive to happiness. That which increases happiness and lessens pain is good; that which does the opposite is evil. Hence it is external forces rather than intuitive perceptions of good or evil which determine moral choices. . . .

For many years [Twain's] works would show that even though strongly attracted to the utilitarian position, he did not wholly accept it. The "discussion with Lecky" would continue for most of his life.

One of the matters on which Clemens partly agreed with

Lecky at this time concerned the nature of the conscience. The historian agreed with the intuitionist view that the conscience was an "original faculty," arising from man's innate perceptions of good and evil. The utilitarians, on the other hand, regarded it simply as an "association of ideas" based on the pleasure-pain theory and society's standards of right and wrong.

To show the inadequacy of the utilitarian concept, Lecky argues that the operation of the conscience does not really fit the view that "self-interest" is the one ultimate reason for virtue. What one "ought or ought not" to do cannot depend merely upon "the prospect of acquiring or losing pleasure." For, if a man had a tendency toward a certain vice, he might well attain happiness by a "moderate and circumspect" indulgence of that vice. But if he sins, his conscience judges his conduct, and "its sting or its approval constitutes a pain or pleasure so intense, as to more than redress the balance." This would happen whether the conscience were an "association of ideas" or "an original faculty."

But (the argument continues) conscience is more often a source of pain than of pleasure, and if happiness is actually the sole end of life, then one should learn to disregard the proddings of conscience. If a man forms an association of ideas that inflicts more pain than it prevents, or prevents more pleasure than it affords, the reasonable course would be to dissolve that association or destroy the habit. "This is what he 'ought' to do according to the only meaning that word can possess in the utilitarian vocabulary." Therefore, a man who possessed such a temperament would be happier if he were to "quench that conscientious feeling, which . . . prevents him from pursuing the course that would be most conducive to his tranquillity.". . .

THE ROLE OF EDUCATION

The second major concept derived from Lecky involves the interrelationship of imagination and compassion, and the influence of education upon both. Shortly after his analysis of the two conflicting moral theories, the historian devotes a long passage to explaining how society's progress from barbarism to a high degree of civilization had depended upon "the strengthening of the imagination by intellectual culture." Defining imagination as "the power of realisation," he argues that men pity suffering only when they "realise" it,

and that the intensity of their compassion is directly proportionate to the extent of that "realisation." That is why the
death of an individual "brought prominently before our eyes"
elicits greater compassion than any account of battle, shipwreck, or other catastrophe. Therefore, if benevolent feelings
thus depend upon prior "realisation," then any influence that
can increase the range and power of the imagination (the "realising faculty") will help to develop sympathy and compassion. And of all such influences, education is the foremost.

Besides the echo in Clemens' letter to Howells, that idea
finds a direct statement early in *The Prince and the Pauper*
when Edward vows (in Chapter Four) to make Christ's Hospital a school for "mental nourishment" rather than "mere
shelter" so that poor boys may develop the "gentleness and
charity" which education encourages. More important, the
concept underlies the subsequent education of Edward and,
in some measure, that of Tom Canty.

EDWARD'S EDUCATION AS CENTRAL THEME

The plot structure of this most carefully wrought of
Clemens' works shows that the author clearly intended Edward's "education" to be primary. Each of the boys gets almost equal space until the end of Chapter Thirteen. But then
the spotlight begins to focus on Edward, as Miles Hendon
discovers the disappearance of his protégé, who has been
lured from the lodgings on London Bridge by a mysterious
message from John Canty. After three chapters describing
Tom's experiences at court following the death of Henry
VIII, the next twelve are Edward's (save for the two that relate Hendon's family troubles). Of the final five, two are
again Tom's; one is shared; the fourth is largely Edward's;
and the unnumbered "Conclusion" briefly summarizes the
subsequent careers of the principal characters, with emphasis on Edward's good works as king.

Prince Edward's schooling begins immediately upon his
ejection from the palace grounds when the group of boys
from Christ's Hospital mock and beat him. His promise to
make the institution into a school, like his initial befriending
of Tom Canty, springs from his own innate "gentleness and
charity." But he is to achieve real compassion and understanding only near the end of his wanderings. As [Twain
critic] Franklin Rogers has noted, when Edward first leaves
the city via London Bridge, he is still an arrogant aristocrat.

He has demanded all the niceties of court etiquette from Miles Hendon and has sworn to have Tom Canty hanged, drawn, and quartered for usurping his throne. Only gradually does the basic soundness of heart, which Hendon recognizes as "the sweet and generous spirit that is in him" assert itself. Finally, after the burning of the Baptist women who befriended him, Edward (in Chapter Twenty-seven) declares that the horror will remain in his memory and his dreams for the rest of his life. Hendon then underscores the change of character by noting how gentle Edward has become; earlier he "would have stormed at these varlets, and said he was king, and commanded that the women be turned loose unscathed."

Other inhumanities in the prison complete the educational process, and Edward swears he will amend the harsh legal code, concluding: "The world is made wrong, kings should go to school to their own laws at times, and so learn mercy." Now he is ready to re-cross London Bridge, a merciful monarch. Subsequently, in righting earlier wrongs, he often stresses the importance of his personal experience, subduing objections by reminding his courtiers that *they* know little of suffering and oppression. And recognizing the tendency of human beings to forget important lessons, he often repeated his story so as to "keep its sorrowful spectacles fresh in his memory and the springs of pity replenished in his heart."

Besides paralleling Lecky's description of the "realisation" process, then, Edward's development reveals a "soundness" of heart like that of Huck Finn. From the first instinctive kindness to Tom, through the sloughing off of the aristocratic arrogance engendered by his upbringing, he proceeds to a conscious kindness. Had he not been innately good, however, it is more than likely that the abuse and ridicule to which his travels exposed him would have far outweighed his pity for the sufferings of others.

Tom Canty's Education

To say that *The Prince and the Pauper* is chiefly Edward's story should not, of course, minimize the importance of Tom Canty's "education." In the first place, once Tom loses his fear of being found out, he begins to discover how false were his dreams of kingly pleasures. Concern over the impending execution of Norfolk, the embarrassment of his first court dinner, and the tedium of business and ceremony successively engulf him until, in Chapter Fourteen, he almost begs to be freed from the "affliction" of kingship. Soon, however, his innately kind heart and sound common sense allow him to initiate a slight amelioration of the harsh laws.

Faced with the prospect of the execution of the alleged poisoner and the two "witches charged with controlling the weather" (Chapter Fifteen), he reacts with instinctive compassion. As Roger Salomon has observed, he faces something of the same conflict of heart and society-trained conscience as both Huck Finn and the historical Edward VI portrayed by David Hume. Of Edward, Hume says that training and "the age in which he lived" qualified his "mildness of disposition" and his "capacity to learn and judge," and thus caused him to "incline somewhat to bigotry and persecution." In a case involving the supposed heresy of a young girl, for instance, the king at first reacted compassionately, refusing to sanction the execution. But his advisers prevailed, and he finally signed the death warrant, though "with tears in his eyes."

Tom Canty, as king, finds himself in a similar position. Like Hume's Edward he is sympathetic. Then, though he grants the "poisoner's" request to be hanged rather than boiled to death, he considers the seriousness of the crime and says with a sigh, "Take him away—he hath earned his death." Fortunately, he decides to review the case further, and when additional questioning reveals the flimsiness of the evidence, reason enters the picture, and Tom frees the man. In the case of the alleged witches, the "influence of the age" again is evident in Tom's superstitious shudder at their presence, a reaction natural in a time when everyone dreaded encountering those possessed by the devil. But whereas the real Edward consented to the execution of the young girl, in this case Tom's sound heart and common sense (again like Huck's) triumph over his trained conscience. Sorry for their plight, Tom reasons that a mother would do anything to save her child, and so offers them freedom and his own protection if they will repeat their magic. When they still protest their inability to create a thunderstorm, he pronounces them innocent and dismisses the charge.

INTUITIVE APPROACH TO CONSCIENCE

Yet those episodes also affect Tom adversely. On realizing that his word truly *is* law, he begins to relish his position and power. Periodically, however, he is plagued by a different sort of conscience—more akin to what Lecky would call an "original" faculty than a community-trained "association of ideas." Tom's shame and guilt arise from two sources: the knowledge that he is usurping Edward's rightful place and his fear that his mother or sisters might appear to thwart his pleasure by exposing him. Though he almost succeeds in following Lecky's advice to quell a troublesome conscience, his guilty feelings continue to torture him. When his pride finally leads him to reject his mother during the coronation procession, all the glamor of kingship falls away as remorse overwhelms him. Edward's appearance in Westminster Abbey brings welcome relief, and Tom is only too glad to relinquish the throne.

One might argue that here Clemens has accorded a purely utilitarian function to the conscience; that Tom's restoring the throne to its rightful occupant and himself to his own family is an action that will ultimately result in the greatest happiness for himself. So it does. But his feelings evolve basically from his natural goodness—his concern for Edward and his love for his family, rather than from a fear of the consequences of being exposed. The miseries of conscience which destroy his happiness and make him glad to give up the throne reflect the kindness and gentleness that he exhibited even at the height of his pleasure in his kingly position. Thus Clemens still seems to side with Lecky.

SUPERSTITION AND FEAR

From Lecky's discussion of the influences of superstition in human affairs at least [one] other episode derived support, if not [its] original inspiration. In Chapter Seventeen, Edward learns of the sad plight of certain husbandmen and of the once-prosperous farmer, Yokel, whose property has been confiscated because his mother was convicted of witchcraft. In a sarcastic harangue to [John Canty's rogue companion] Hugo's outlaw band, Yokel describes his experiences with "the merciful English law": when he had turned to begging as his only recourse, he had for successive offenses been whipped, deprived of both ears, branded, and finally enslaved. "Do ye understand that word!" he shouts; "An English SLAVE!" And then he explains that he has fled from his master and, if caught, will hang.

At that point the horrified Edward cries that the law shall be revoked that very day, whereupon he is robed, crowned, sceptered, and dubbed "Foo-Foo the First, King of the Moon-calves." To keep the historical record straight, the author contributes a note to this passage which explains that the peasant was "suffering from this law *by anticipation,*" for the statute "was to have birth in this little king's own reign." But, he adds, "we know, from the humanity of his character, that it could never have been suggested by him." Presumably, this law was to be among those which Edward (in the novel) would later repeal. . . .

REFORM OF THE INDIVIDUAL NOT THE MONARCHY

In some respects Clemens' attacks on superstition point to-ward *A Connecticut Yankee,* where Lecky was to play an even larger role. Edward's travels among his people, too, foreshadow the similar journey of King Arthur. Neverthe-less, many commentators have read *The Prince and the Pau-per* under too strong a glow from *A Connecticut Yankee.* [Twain critic Bernard] DeVoto's conclusion, for instance, that the author was attacking as much as he could manage of the "modern perpetuation" of the harsh Tudor law, is war-ranted neither by Clemens' political and social attitudes at the time of composition nor by the book itself. First, the novel was conceived when Clemens' admiration for En-gland, her traditions, and her government was at its zenith. At that time he may well have thought of the many examples of religious persecution and severe treatment of prisoners (gathered mainly from Hume in 1877) as "local color" which would illustrate the hardships to be observed by the little king in contrast to the "horrible miseries of princedom" to be borne by Tom Canty. Nor had his conviction of the com-mon man's incompetence in government changed much as a result of the European trip of 1878–79. Nowhere in his per-sonal utterances of these years, nor in *The Prince and the Pauper* itself, is there any sign of his later contention that all monarchies should be overthrown. Tudor law was oppres-sive, to be sure, and bespoke a system sorely deficient in re-spect for human rights. But it was man rather than monar-chy that needed reform; first the rulers and then the people themselves must be rid of false notions. DeVoto's suggested title, "A Missouri Democrat at the Court of Edward VI" is thus inaccurate, and ascribes ideas to Clemens that he demonstrably did not hold when he wrote the book.

In the book itself there is relatively little satire of monarchy and aristocracy. The sharpest thrusts at court ceremony occur in the ludicrous picture of grown men stumbling and fumbling as they attempt to clothe one small boy. Balanced against this sort of burlesque is an obvious fascination with the traditional pomp and display associated with other ceremonies, such as the coronation. Even in the exposure of the more striking legal atrocities of the age, Clemens' target is not the iniquity of the system which produced them but the ignorance and superstition of the age.

No Egalitarian Message

Finally, . . . the often-cited picture of Tom and Edward standing naked before a mirror, amazed at their identical appearances, cannot really be read as proof of Clemens' current belief in social or political equality. Barring the fact that the plot itself demanded such physical similarity, other evidence seriously weakens any argument that Clemens had freighted *The Prince and the Pauper* with an "equalitarian" message. In fact, when the novel was in full swing and nearing completion in August, 1880, the author was planning still another episode for *Captain Stormfield's Visit to Heaven* with opposite implications. As the notebook sketch indicates, Stormfield was first to be charmed with the idea that the residents of Paradise lived in a world completely free of social barriers. But when a Negro, a Fiji Islander, an Eskimo, and various politicians, tramps, and other pariahs began inviting themselves to dinner and calling him "Brother Stormfield," he was to grow progressively less enthusiastic. Finally, he would become disgusted by this enforced association with "all sorts of disagreeable people," and would resolve to move from heaven. Such a plan, though not ultimately used, shows that Clemens in 1880 and 1881 had not deviated far from his social and political opinions of the 1870's.

Moral Education of Rulers

The "message" of *The Prince and the Pauper*, then, was not that British monarchy was evil, not even that monarchy in itself breeds injustice. It was rather that the cure for political and social ills might be achieved through the paternalistic rule of those best qualified to rule, whose qualifications should include innate kindness, intelligence, and the "realisation" provided by "education." The book is much closer to "The Curious Republic of Gondour" with its mistrust of the masses and plea for qualified public officials, or to *Huckle-berry Finn* with its belief in the efficacy of the "sound heart," than to the Yankee Hank Morgan's proposal to demolish and then recreate on an equalitarian basis the institutions of a nation. Nevertheless, its exposure of ignorance, superstition, and unreason does reflect a further deepening of Clemens' disillusionment with human nature. And the careers of its protagonists show Clemens a step closer to the proposition that environment and circumstances alone determine the course of life.

Though Clemens thus weighted *The Prince and the Pauper* with serious implications, the novel unfortunately fails to transcend the limitations of time, place, and melodramatic action. Hence, it lacks the universality which allows *Huckleberry Finn*, or even *Tom Sawyer*, to grip the minds and imaginations of adult readers. The book continues to be read, certainly, but its appeal is chiefly to children and to students of Clemens' literary development, rather than to "young people of all ages."

CHAPTER 4

The Issue of Identity

Fathers and Sons

John Daniel Stahl

Much of the focus of contemporary criticism of Mark Twain has been on analyzing his works to see what they reveal about the inner dilemmas and psychological conflicts of Samuel Clemens. From this perspective *The Prince and the Pauper* has been the subject of renewed critical interest, with the consensus being that the novel is more enlightening about Clemens and more closely related to American concerns than was previously believed. In the following article John Daniel Stahl, of Virginia State University, says *The Prince and the Pauper* represents the American myth of the son in search of a father disguised in a European setting. Stahl says the relationship between fathers and sons and issues of inheritance deeply concerned Samuel Clemens. He draws parallels with Clemens's life following the early death of his father and claims that American males of every generation face the problem of creating and selecting new father figures. In the process they develop their own resources and establish a unique identity. Stahl, an American who grew up in Europe, has been drawn to the study of Twain's European novels in a personal quest to gain clarity on his own sense of identity as an American male.

Tom H. Towers has argued in a 1978 article that *The Prince and the Pauper* is "a major and forthright expression of a cultural and political conservatism which is a minor note in Twain's writing." Towers interprets this conservatism as the obverse of his "despairing contempt" for human civilization. Kenneth Andrews has similarly stressed the origin of the novel in the genteel values and literary tastes of Nook Farm, the elite Hartford neighborhood where Samuel Clemens made his home in the 1870s and 80s. The growing hostility

Excerpted from "American Myth in European Disguise: Fathers and Sons in *The Prince and the Pauper*," by John Daniel Stahl, *American Literature*, May 1986. Copyright © 1986 by Duke University Press. Reprinted with permission from Duke University Press.

towards England and in particular towards British critics of America that Twain expressed vehemently in the 1880s was still mild and largely unarticulated at the time he wrote *The Prince and the Pauper.* This is not to say, however, that Twain's historical romance was a comfortable concession to the dominant cultural tenor of respectable New England society, as many critics have claimed. Recent critics' treatment of the book has frequently tended to be a sophisticated version of Van Wyck Brooks' old thesis: the artist was intimidated into curtailing his criticisms of society, or acquiesced in their suppression. In this view, he sold the honesty of his vision, partially expressed in *Adventures of Huckleberry Finn,* for a mess of pottage.

MARK TWAIN AS THWARTED GENIUS

The dualism of this approach to Twain is exacerbated by a tendency to treat his works of the late 1870s and early 80s almost as if they had been written by two different authors. The hack writer competes with the literary genius, in this view. In *Huck Finn* the latter won, mostly, this theory holds; in *The Prince and the Pauper* the former has the upper hand. This tendency is further encouraged by the requirement of literary history that it focus upon prophetic and groundbreaking works. *The Prince and the Pauper* represents little if any departure from conventional forms and styles, while Hemingway's statement that all modern American literature comes from one book does not sound preposterous any more. Another dimension of the duality addressed here is that *Huck Finn* records an era of American history, while *The Prince and the Pauper* is set in the distant European past. Furthermore, *The Prince and the Pauper* has frequently been dismissed as a children's book, while critics take satisfaction in suggesting complexities in *Huck Finn* that are beyond the comprehension of a child audience. This ignores, among other things, Clemens' subtitle for *The Prince and the Pauper,* which is "A Tale for Young People of All Ages."

Mark Twain's own overestimation of the literary value of his Tudor romance appears to have contributed to its denigration by twentieth-century critics. This is due in part to the resounding victory of critics such as H.L. Mencken in the battle of naturalism against gentility and romanticism in American letters. As Arthur L. Vogelback has described, *The Prince and the Pauper* "fitted in perfectly with the tradition of correctness and imitation—with the genteel tradition" and was praised accordingly by contemporary critics, including Clemens' friend William Dean Howells. The novel's lack of originality and innovation is presumably part of what Leonard Woolf reacted against when he condemned the work as betraying "a commonness and tawdriness, a lack of sensitiveness, which do not matter to the impetuous appetite of youth, but which cannot be ignored by the more discriminating and exacting taste of middle-age." However, the consensus of recent critical assessment has missed a significant dimension of meaning in *The Prince and the Pauper.* This meaning resides in the realm where the themes of Mark Twain's psychological obsessions and his quest for a cultural identity meet.

Despite critics' tendency to dismiss *The Prince and the Pauper*, it deserves serious attention, both as a story that has proven its durability with readers over more than a century and as a significant part of Mark Twain's oeuvre. Though the fact that it is Mark Twain's most carefully plotted novel may not count in its favor artistically by contemporary standards, it is a mistake to discount it entirely in a consideration of Mark Twain's development as an artist.

FATHER-SON RELATIONSHIPS IN TWAIN NOVELS

The European setting that the aspiring young journalist Mark Twain had employed as a comic backdrop for self-dramatization in *Innocents Abroad* served the established, middle-aged father Samuel Clemens as the context for his story of fatherless sons seeking an identity and an inheritance through surrogate fathers. The period between 1877 and 1880 was a time when Mark Twain reached beyond the relatively tame world of the fatherless Tom Sawyer into the imaginative inner life of Huck Finn, who escapes the grasp of his savage, destructive father. *The Prince and the Pauper* abounds with symbolic father-son relationships that are curiously paradoxical in ways that form a significant contrast to *Huck Finn.* Robert Regan and Albert E. Stone, Jr., have commented, in different ways, on the significance of the father-son relationships in the former work. What has not been developed is why and how the European setting freed Mark Twain to write about father-son relationships as a dynamic possibility within a society. Neither *The Adventures of Tom Sawyer* nor *Adventures of Huckleberry Finn* offered this possibility in quite such a form, though Tom Sawyer, Huckleberry Finn, Tom Canty, and Edward all have in common that they are or become orphans in one way or another. Tom Sawyer's father is never mentioned, Huck's father Pap dies early in *Huck Finn* (though Huck does not find it out until the end), Tom Canty's father runs away at the end of the book and is never heard from again, and Edward's father Henry VIII's death is of course central to the plot.

The legacy of beneficent surrogate fathers combined with the strength and efforts of the natural selves of the heroes in *The Prince and the Pauper* creates a better life for the boys and for their society. While for Tom Sawyer and Huck Finn, imaginative expansion and education about social roles through European or pseudo-European models lead ultimately back to where they started from, a relationship to society that has not essentially changed, what Tom Canty and the Prince of Wales learn about social roles in the midst of symbolic European institutions leads to redefined relationships to their society, and even to relatively small but nonetheless significant changes in that society itself. "The reign of Edward VI was a singularly merciful one for those harsh times," Mark Twain states in the final paragraph. He implies that the improvement of justice under Edward's rule was prophetic of greater progress in that direction made in later centuries, an ameliorative tendency that places his "tale for young people of all ages" squarely in the genteel tradition of literature for youth written by authors such as his neighbor Harriet Beecher Stowe and Charlotte M. Yonge.

THE DREAMS OF TWAIN'S MAJOR CHARACTERS

The conflict between social circumstances and the inner lives and aspirations of his characters is a theme that appears in *Huck Finn* and in *The Prince and the Pauper.* Twain's version of European customs, institutions, and historical events represents a utopian / dystopian world of grand hopes and cruel, amoral realities. The utopian aspect of Twain's Europe is its capacity to represent dream-objects of desire. For Tom Canty, the dream-object is a life of grandeur, luxury, and comfort as a prince, while Tom Sawyer interestingly enough aspires to a parody of such a life. Twain treats Canty's aspiration seriously, though it has some comic consequences, whereas he treats Tom Sawyer's aspiration comically, though it has some serious consequences (such as the diminution of

Jim's dignity and significance). For Edward, Prince of Wales, the dream-object is to play without rules or boundaries, social or geographical, a freedom of the sort that Huck Finn attains, but only too briefly. In both cases, Twain shows us some of the costs of the desire for freedom. For Miles Hendon, as for Jim in *Huck Finn,* the dream-object is more poignantly adult: to return home after a long absence, to rejoin the love of his youth, and to gain his share of the inheritance which is rightfully his (in Jim's case, to gain possession of himself—his freedom).

AMERICAN MYTH IN EUROPEAN DISGUISE

The Prince and the Pauper clearly contains a strand of mythic story, both in [sociologist Emil] Durkheim's sense of myth as "allegorical introduction, to shape the individual to his group" and in the Jungian interpretation of myth as "group dream, symptomatic of archetypal urges within the depths of the human psyche." The cruelty of certain incidents in the story reinforces the mythic, folk-tale-like quality of parts of the novel. For example, there is the hermit's sharpening his knife to butcher the bound boy, or the burning of the Baptist women at the stake. . . .

Twain's orphaned sons seek to accomplish the impossible: to recover their lost fathers; and in the process they invent themselves. *The Prince and the Pauper* reveals the extent to which, even in his minor works, Mark Twain's obsessions coincided with the cultural preoccupations of his countrymen. In *The Prince and the Pauper,* the teleology of the New World individual's psychology and the mythos of American identity merge, given shape yet also disguised by the European setting.

CHARACTERS AS SYMBOLS

Europe in *The Prince and the Pauper* is a mythopoetic realm of symbolic social extremes and of fairy-tale-like father-son relationships. His characters are all supposedly English, and the action is supposed to have taken place in the real, if fictionalized, past of sixteenth-century England. His central character is an historical figure: the prince and later boy-king Edward VI. But as authentic as details of the setting and story are, the essential force of the story is mythic and the perspective from which the story is told is distinctly American. Mark Twain's sixteenth-century London is intrinsically a fantasy realm like that of the fairy-tale, in which heart's desires are more important than quotidian reality. Kingship and pauperdom are significant here not primarily as historical facts but as metaphors for social and personal conditions, conditions from which each boy, prince and pauper, imagines escape. The characters of prince and pauper are stylized into complementary compatibility, making an exchange of roles possible. Each boy is inherently noble and imaginative, the prince of necessity brave and strong enough to meet his misadventures among the rabble, the pauper wise enough to meet the challenges of life at court. But each boy also requires the aid of a benevolent father-figure.

Mark Twain opposes their natural, authentic characters to the artificialities and cruelties of a Manichaean Europe. In the struggle to regain their social identities, each of the three main characters, Tom Canty, Edward, Prince of Wales, and Miles Hendon (each of the three in some sense a boy), realizes his authentic self, which in the end proves to be as important as the social identity he lost. Though Edward becomes king, Miles regains his inheritance, and Tom Canty is appointed to the post of chief governor of Christ's Hospital, these destinies are not as important as the proving of their authentic characters that each goes through.

The American nature of Twain's treatment of his special European material becomes clear when one examines his themes closely. The centrality of natural character, particularly in the person of innocent Tom Canty at court, but also in the spontaneous responses and positive inner resources of Miles Hendon and Edward, both in manners and in moral questions, suggests the continuity of Europe and America in Mark Twain's imagination at this time. The ultimate aim of each son is to regain his identity, which is initially the identity conferred upon him by being his particular father's son. Though Tom Canty does not desire to claim an identity related to his father's, he does have to renounce an identity based on being the son of a man who is not his father, and he aspires to an identity revealed to him by his surrogate father. Tom Canty represents the outcast seeking to establish a place for himself in a stratified society. The circumstances he is thrown into, which range from extreme poverty and abuse to the pinnacle of wealth and power, present him with tests of character in which he must conduct himself well in order to attain a state in which his inner character is manifest and acknowledged through his social role, a theme consonant with the "rags to riches" genre of American writing.

ORPHANHOOD AND INHERITANCE

The symbolic American individual is multiply represented in *The Prince and the Pauper* by the disinherited son, the son who is actually or practically orphaned, reflecting the preoccupation with orphanhood shared by American writers such as Horatio Alger and Frances Hodgson Burnett. Orphanhood, one might argue, is a characteristically American condition; for a nation of immigrants and uprooted persons, losing parents is a common, symbolically potent experience. [Sociologist] Oscar Handlin has poignantly discussed the loss of parental authority and of continuity between the generations among immigrant families, even when children have not literally become orphans. The father-figures in *Huck Finn* and *Tom Sawyer* are not in a position to bestow a place in society on their sons. Jim, the adult to whom Huck is closest, of course cannot do so because he is a slave. Except for a certain resourcefulness that encompasses trickery and self-serving rationalization, Pap has no legacy except cruelty, prejudice, and anarchy to offer his son. . . . The historical romance provided Mark Twain with a context in which he could envision generational succession in positive terms. Whereas in *Huck Finn* his characters develop an authentic self at the cost of social position or a social position at the cost of the authentic self, Tom Canty and Edward are able to achieve both.

While *The Prince and the Pauper* is also circular in the sense that Edward and Miles return to their original social positions (while Tom moves from pauperdom to a comfortable sinecure), in the book with the European setting Mark Twain imagined multiple father-son relationships that issue in a form of generational succession. The paradox is that in this American form of inheritance the son has to win the right to inherit his father's legacy and even, in one case, becomes his father's symbolic father. Twain implies that the aid a father can give is only equal to or less than the inner resources a son must have to achieve his goals.

PARALLELS WITH TWAIN'S LIFE

It is only on the literal level true, as Albert E. Stone, Jr., claims, that Mark Twain's historical romance is "not in the least autobiographical in origin." Even on the literal level, coincidences between this story which Mark Twain took such satisfaction in writing and his own life point to psychological, symbolic autobiography. Mark Twain was eleven years and several months old when his father, John Clemens, died. Though the historical Edward was nine years old when Henry VIII died, Mark Twain asked that "the artist always picture the Prince & Tom Canty as lads of 13 or 14 years old." Thus the historical and the fictional Edwards' ages bracket Sam Clemens' age at the time of his father's death, indicating a probable correspondence between the position of the semi-fictional boy at his father's death and Clemens' own experience. Furthermore, John Clemens was a judge; judges figure prominently in *The Prince and the Pauper.* Henry VIII appears in the role of judge when he condemns the Duke of Norfolk to execution, and other characters act as judges in the story as well: Tom Canty in the role of the Prince hears and decides the cases of several of his subjects, and a justice of the peace presides as judge in the case against Edward when he is accused of stealing a dressed pig.

TRIPLE FATHER FIGURES

Without wishing to overstress the autobiographical implications of these parallels, I do wish to point to the very prominent emphasis given to father-son relationships in *The Prince and the Pauper* and to the bearing which these relationships have on the idea of inheritance. The transmission of the story itself is attributed to story-telling from father to son, as indicated in the prefatory note:

> I will set down a tale as it was told to me by one who had it of his father, which latter had it of *his* father, this last having in like manner had it of *his* father—and so on, back and still back, three hundred years and more, the fathers transmitting it to the sons and so preserving it.

The story itself represents a legacy handed down from father to son, for many generations, in a stylized fashion that is reminiscent of the oral transmission of fairy tales. This is appropriate, for the story needs to be read on one level as a fairy tale of good, evil, and Manichaean good-and-evil father-figures. The mythic import of the story is that each son has a configuration of three father-figures, ranging from good to evil, each son is thrust into a society which denies

his identity as his physical father's son, and he must regain
that identity but do it largely out of his own resources. For
example, Tom Canty has three symbolic fathers. His physical father, John Canty, a version of Pap Finn, is ignorant,
brutish, and cruel. He beats his son and exploits him in
every way he can. He is a drunkard and a representative of
the dregs of society. Tom's spiritual father, in more than the
religious sense, his good father, is the kindly, elderly priest,
Father Andrew, who has been forced into retirement on a
scant pension by a harsh edict of Henry VIII. The priest
teaches the boy Latin and introduces him to the romance of
folk tales and the world of old books. By doing so, he provides the boy with means of escape from the ugly, narrow
confines of his day-to-day life of begging, starvation, and
physical abuse. Once he is at court, he meets another of his
father-figures: the aged King Henry, an awesome personage
to little Tom Canty, but someone who treats him with kindness and indulgence, despite the real prince's statement that
his father did not always spare him with his tongue, and that
he had "not a doll's temper." Henry soon dies, and John
Canty, significantly, kills the one man in Offal Court who
pleads for Tom / Edward when the boy appears to have lost
his mind: Father Andrew. Thus, symbolically, the cruel father kills the kind father and Tom is left to fend for himself.
Tom has to act out of his own resources and impulses at
court. As in the ordeal formula common to the genteel fiction of the period, his innate gifts prove largely adequate to
the challenge of the circumstances he must face. However,
Twain's narrative is distinct from typical ordeal formula fiction in that there is no permanent return to the safety of
adult protection possible. . . .

GOOD VERSUS EVIL FATHERS

The pattern that emerges in the connections between the father figures is that of competition and conflict between the
good and the evil father figures. The evil fathers struggle to
control their sons, while the good fathers are repeatedly
powerless to protect the boys. John Canty kills Father Andrew; Hugh Hendon jails Miles; the protective father Henry
dies, leaving both sons to their fates. If one looks for similar
patterns in *Huck Finn*, the striking fact is that none of the potential father figures (except Jim) is ultimately benevolent:
certainly not Pap, nor Colonel Grangerford, Sherburn, or

even Silas Phelps, who contributes to setting an armed mob at the heels of the fleeing heroes. . . . Both books convey the nightmarish aura of threat that emanates from powerful adult males. However, in *The Prince and the Pauper*, that threat is sometimes mitigated by the good father figures, who are, however, temporarily deprived of social legitimation. Edward's most significant relationship to a father-figure, for example, resembling Huck's with Jim, is with Miles Hendon, the boyish, good-hearted soldier who is himself in a predicament parallel to Edward's. Miles must establish his identity in order to reclaim his rightful inheritance. . . . Miles' rightful inheritance is finally restored to him through the power of the boy who has been his symbolic son and becomes his symbolic father: Edward. As king, Edward is Miles' sovereign and lord. That Edward is much younger than Miles, and that Miles protected him in dangerous circumstances, makes no difference to that fact.

CENTRAL THEME OF INHERITANCE

Metaphorically, one might argue, the central question of *The Prince and the Pauper* is the one which Tom Canty cannot repress when he hears that his "father," King Henry VIII, will not be buried right away but instead in several days: "Will he keep?" What the question implies, metaphorically, is a central theme of the book, and an enduring American concern: what qualities, good or bad, will sons inherit from their fathers? What of their fathers will keep? Will their fathers keep? The literal meaning of the question echoes the concern of fairy-tale characters to preserve dead bodies until they can be transformed or laid to rest (cf. "Snow White" or "The Juniper Tree," for example). Yet the mythic dimension is rooted in the author's life. The well-known circumstance of young Sam Clemens' witnessing his father's postmortem through a keyhole sheds further light on the significance to Mark Twain of the painful question of the physical destruction of the father's body after death. . . .

FINDING NEW FATHERS AT THE HEART OF AMERICAN CULTURE

In the remoteness of sixteenth-century England, . . . [Twain found a] stimulant for writing about father-son inheritance and the problematic nature of succession in a characteristically American way. Mark Twain's boyish heroes must largely fend for themselves, and their innate qualities are better than their society's values. . . . He conceives the European past in *The Prince and the Pauper* as a mythic world of cruelty, injustice, and artificiality, but also of grandeur and hope. Boys whose hearts are still natural find themselves confronted with a stratified society that denies their social identity, their parentage. In seeking to reclaim that identity, they develop instead an authentic one, for which they require the aid of substitute fathers. Their physical fathers fail them, socially and personally. Their only genuine legacy, as in *Huck Finn*, lies in their own resources: character, and the companionship they offer one another. Even in the sixteenth-century England Mark Twain imagined, fathers will not keep. For Mark Twain, as for Americans of every generation, new fathers must be found. Samuel Clemens not only created Mark Twain, he invented his own version of the myth of the boy who creates and selects his own father. As I hope to have shown, his invention of new fathers in *The Prince and the Pauper* is not as far from the deepest impulses of his art as has been supposed.

The Impostor Phenomenon

Jerry Griswold

In the following excerpt from *Audacious Kids: Coming of Age in America's Children's Classic Books* (1992), Jerry Griswold, professor of American Literature at San Diego State University, analyzes *The Prince and the Pauper* from a psychological and psychohistorical perspective. He claims the novel is of the caliber of *The Adventures of Huckleberry Finn* and more revealing of the inner life of Samuel Clemens than any other work by Mark Twain. Griswold says Twain's handling of the symmetrical patterns of Tom and Edward's stories is brilliant. He describes the "Impostor Phenomenon," which is the anxiety of people who though genuine, feel as if they are impostors. He claims this theme is evident in the novel, Twain's fiction in general and reflects Clemens's personal anxiety given his meteoric rise from his poor background to life among elite social groups. According to Griswold, unlike *Huckleberry Finn* which celebrates America's newfound independence from Europe, *The Prince and the Pauper* has themes of continuity and succession, reflecting a national anxiety in the post Revolutionary War period about being orphaned, disowned, and disinherited.

Over the years, psychologists have studied the personality of the impostor—those individuals whose stories occasionally appear in the newspapers after they have masqueraded as, for example, policemen or doctors. In recent years, however, psychologists have recognized another, related malady that they have named "the impostor phenomenon." This is a debilitating anxiety of individuals who feel *as if* they are impostors: the successful trial lawyer who worries that he will be exposed as a phony on some elementary point of law; the computer programmer who is fearful of the mistake that will show others that he has just been faking it; the middle-aged person who believes that she is still a child and only pretending to be an adult; the student who gets good grades but is still troubled about the exam that will reveal she is actually a dunce.

Visions of both the genuine impostor (if that is the right term) and the impostor phenomenon are present throughout *The Prince and the Pauper.* In the first case, Edward Tudor is thought to be an impostor when he claims to be the prince; Miles Hendon is wrongly accused of being an impostor when he claims to be himself; John Canty (a master at disguises) often pretends to be someone other than he is; and eventually Tom Canty has to be an impostor and play at being the monarch until the real one is found. But it is really in terms of the impostor phenomenon that much of *The Prince and the Pauper* can be understood. What baffles many of the characters in the book is Tom Canty's continual insistence that he is not the prince; as one of the royal ministers observes, "Now were he impostor and called himself prince, look you that would be natural; that would be reasonable. But lived ever an impostor yet, who, being called prince by the king, . . . denied all his dignity and pleaded against his exaltation!"

Generally speaking, victims of the impostor phenomenon are frequently individuals who find themselves in new circumstances, often through sudden and unanticipated success: the executive, for example, who is suddenly promoted to the top echelons and thinks, "I'm really just a kid from the streets who used to play stickball, so I'll have to fake it." The malady that results may be said to have four pronounced characteristics: first, a conviction of a split between a "true" self and a "false" self; second, guilt about this discrepancy, about being a "hypocrite"; third, a terrible need to hide a "secret" identity; and, finally, an acute fear of exposure—real insecurity and genuine worry about unpredictable situations that might result in humiliation, particularly social situations in which some accident might occur that would bring the hoax down like a house of cards.

To readers familiar with *The Prince and the Pauper*, the applicability of these concepts to Tom Canty's situation may already be apparent. He constantly feels a discrepancy between his "true" and "false" identities; for example, he "tried hard to acquit himself satisfactorily, but he was too new to such things, and too ill at ease to accomplish more than a tolerable success. He looked sufficiently like a king, but he was ill able to feel like one." And Tom has the impostor's anxiety about being exposed and worries that some sudden event will topple the edifice of his charade. This only makes him feel more acutely that he is a fake and a hypocrite. . . .

HUMILIATION AND SHAME

But more than anything else, what signals the presence of the impostor's anxieties is the fact that throughout the book the most acute pain comes from humiliation or the fear of it. This is a novel in which hurt is inflicted publicly through jeering, shaming, and ridicule. Poor Tom is jeered by crowds when he comes in his rags to see the castle. After the exchange of clothes, a mob hoots at Prince Edward, and later he is ragged by charity children. While in regal habiliment, Tom worries that the servants are sneering at him behind his back. Recalling the mockery Christ suffered, Edward suffers his own mock coronation and public ridicule at the hands of taunting vagabonds unable to stomach his claims to the throne. And when Miles offers to take Edward's place to save him from a public flogging, the boy monarch is grateful for something other than being spared physical injury; such injury, he says, is "less than nothing!—when 'tis weighed against the act of him who saves his prince from SHAME!". . .

PARALLELS WITH CLEMENS'S LIFE

Clemens's own sudden ascendancy—from poor white folks eating cornpone in frontier Missouri to the well-to-do sitting down to china place settings in the gilded parlors of Hartford—provided, no doubt, fertile ground for the particular kinds of fantasies and anxieties that appear in *The Prince and the Pauper*. His own childhood, Clemens explained, was marked by financial reversals. His father was one of the most "honored and opulent citizens of Fentress County" until the crash of 1834 reduced him to a pauper, and he was forced to relocate to Hannibal. There his father slowly rebuilt his fortunes until they were lost once again when he was obliged to honor a loan made by another man who declared bankruptcy. They were paupers, Clemens confessed, living in a muddy little river town. And it was a town infected with "gold fever," since Hannibal was one of the last jumping-off points for get-rich-quick folks headed overland to make their fortunes in the Gold Rush. Mining a similar vein in the evenings, the family enjoyed talking about their vanished grandeur and speculating about their noble ancestors—their kinship with one of the judges of King Charles I, a claim they had on the earlship of Durham.

Clemens's own Cinderella-like ascendancy from barefoot Missouri boy to newspaper royalty was certain to seem a dislocation. Clemens himself not only acknowledged this, but emphasized it: he was a Southerner living in the North, a frontiersman in genteel company, an American in Europe. As others have observed, this sense of "twin" identity is suggested in everything Twain/Clemens did, from the day he coined his doubled moniker [that is, the name of Mark Twain] to his last words on his deathbed, when he mumbled incoherently about Dr. Jekyll and Mr. Hyde.

IMPOSTORS IN TWAIN'S FICTION

These obsessions are reflected in his work: in the fascination with Siamese twins, the exchanged identities of Tom and Huck in the conclusion of *Huckleberry Finn*, the changelings of *Pudd'nhead Wilson*, the transpositions of *The Prince and the Pauper*, and elsewhere. The episode in *Huckleberry Finn* in which two sets of brothers both claim to be related to Peter Wilks is repeated over and over again in Clemens's work: the question is always who is the true and genuine and who is the fraud and impostor.

There may be no other author in the world who can match Clemens in his bona fide obsession with genuineness. His work reveals a consuming preoccupation with frauds, pretenders, con men, hoaxes, dupes, shams, and deceptions. His greatest characters ply this trade: the Duke and the King, Colonel Sellers, and several boys who move in and out of ruses with incredible alacrity. At the beginning of his career, as a journalist in Nevada, Clemens made a name for himself as a perpetrator of hoaxes. At other times, especially late in his life, he seemed to be a Catcher in the Rye eager to preserve others from various fads that he perceived as frauds—be it the Christian Science movement or Sir Walter Scott's novels. . . .

MEMORY AND SUCCESSION

Impostors—who, even into adulthood, persist in the childhood fantasy that they were born of royal parents and who demand their birthright—turn their backs on the facts. In their denial of their actual or genuine past lies a discontinuity of identity. Memory is rejected.

Memory is what makes life successive. And given that the principal concern of *The Prince and the Pauper* is usurpation and the dangers of interrupted succession, it is not surprising that memory plays so large a role in the novel.

The danger Tom Canty faces is that he will forget who he is in his intoxication with his impostrous identity. The satisfactions are considerable. While masquerading as the prince, Tom witnesses how his every wish is a command and how he is universally honored, the Child Regent. In this heady and egocentric atmosphere, as his coronation approaches, he seems ready to unthinkingly embrace the fantasy and forget the facts—but in that way lies madness. Sanity is finally restored, however, during "The Recognition Procession" that precedes the coronation in the book's conclusion. . . .

EDWARD'S MEMORY

Unlike Tom, Edward has the memory of the proverbial elephant. He never forgets who he is. Edward's persistence in this is nothing short of incredible, since it brings him only pain and ridicule from those (like John Canty and the vagabonds) who cannot stomach his assertions that he is actually the prince, or patronizing kindness from those who simply think the boy is crazed. In his insistence, they think him mad, unable to remember who he really is. Even Miles Hendon is surprised by "the grip his memory doth take upon his quaint and crazy fancies."

But it is Edward's strength of memory that brings about his salvation and leads to the improvement of life in England. During his period among his people, Edward constantly exercises his memory, and not just in remembrance of who he really is or in the affairs of court. When he is rudely treated by a group of orphans, he decides that they need learning as well as food and shelter, and he resolves: "I will keep this diligently in my remembrance, that this day's lesson be not lost upon me, and my people suffer thereby." When he is forced to witness Baptist women being burned at the stake, he determines to change the laws when given the chance: "That which I have seen, in that one little moment, will never go out of my memory." And when Miles takes a public flogging originally intended for him, Edward promises to reward his honored subject: "this loyal deed shall never perish out of my memory. I will not forget it!"

Edward's memory receives its most important test, of course, in the resolution of the novel. In front of all the assembled nobles, with the crown of England hanging in the balance, Edward must remember where he hid the Great Seal on the day he and Tom exchanged clothes. Tom encourages him, "Bethink thee, my king—spur thy memory. . . . Recall everything!" And he finally does. Memory puts all things right. The boy who never forgot who he was now ascends the throne. . . .

LARGER AMERICAN CONCERNS

Impostors, problems of succession, . . . the salvific power of memory—what has all this to do with America, and how does it explain the unusual popularity of Clemens's book? Until now, we have, for the most part, been examining Clemens's novel at close range and in a psychological and biographical manner. If we widen our discussion now in a psychohistorical fashion, we can begin to see how Clemens's private concerns echoed larger, cultural concerns. . . .

POLITICAL READINGS OF CHILDREN'S LITERATURE

[A number of children's classics published during the Golden Age critiqued the] European monarchism and advocated the American alternative of natural nobility. This theme is especially conspicuous in *The Prince and the Pauper*. The pauper is a kind and wise ruler for a time because, when he assumes his royal office, he brings with him a heart that has been educated among the people. So, too, the prince becomes a better ruler because of his moral reeducation among hoi polloi. In the same way, Cedric Errol [in *Little Lord Fauntleroy*] makes a benevolent Lord Fauntleroy because he has first been an ordinary kid on the streets of New York. And Tarzan, the offspring of Lord and Lady Greystoke, is all the better because, instead of depending on his nobility, he has had the occasion to descend to the bottom of the evolutionary ladder and (in free competition) prove his mettle in nature and rise to the top.

But we should note a contradiction. In these three American books what is offered is a compromised version of "natural nobility." Except for Tom Canty's brief interlude in *The Prince and the Pauper*, none of these novels tells the democratic story of a prole [working class person] who rises to a position of power. Instead, in each, the hero is nobly born but finds himself in reduced circumstances. In each, the noble child goes through a process of reeducation among the people and then (following the pattern of the Family Romance) resumes his rank in a manner that suggests a reification and renewal of the notion of nobility.

THEMES OF CONTINUITY AND SUCCESSION

In these three novels, in other words, the major emphasis does not fall on the democratic and antipatriarchal rhetoric that marks, say, the exposure of the Wizard as a humbug in *The Wizard of Oz* or the King as naked in *Huckleberry Finn.* To be sure, this is a minor motif in all three. Still, instead of a *break* with the father, *Fauntleroy* and *Tarzan* and *The Prince and the Pauper* are . . . concerned with continuity: with succession, ancestry, and lineage.

This concern is also suggested by the differences between Clemens's companion books, the two he once thought of binding together [*The Prince and the Pauper* and *Huck Finn*]. With the characters of the Duke and the King, for example, *Adventures of Huckleberry Finn* rejects *paternal* impostors, who are both royal pretenders and usurpers of the father's place (when, for example, they falsely claim to be the rightful guardians of the Wilks girls). *The Prince and the Pauper*, in contrast, presents this theme's counterpart, its twain: a concern with *filial* impostors, usurpers of the son's place and rightful birthright. In the second work, in other words, parricidal impulses [subconscious wishes to eradicate the father] are largely absent; they are replaced by the worries of a son—of being bereft, orphaned, disowned. *The Prince and the Pauper*, we might say, addresses post-Revolutionary concerns, ones that arose after America had so forcefully separated from its European parents. While *Huckleberry Finn* celebrates the break with the father, *The Prince and the Pauper* addresses the anxiety that arose after that break had occurred. . . .

In writing this genteel novel, Mark Twain's personal bid for respectability echoed similar national wishes of a mature . . . America. This America wished to emphasize the ancestral. It had seen in the Civil War the dangers of ceaseless oedipal rebellion and wished to emphasize continuity. It was preoccupied (via noted historians George Bancroft and Francis Parkman) with solidifying the country's historicity. It had grown up and settled its antagonism with the fatherland.

THE PRINCE AND THE PAUPER AS "FAKELORE"

This milieu may also explain why Clemens chose the *historical* novel as his genre and why he went to such great and tedious lengths to point repeatedly to his book's fidelity to the facts. The novel begins with an epigraph about the faithful transmission of this story from father to son. As the story proceeds, faithful memory becomes the primary tool for undoing confusion, for separating fantasy from fact. And all along the way, Clemens feels a need to assert the book's historical accuracy. This is a novel with footnotes! It is also full of bibliographical references to the histories Clemens consulted, frequent editorial intrusions meant to indicate to the reader the unusual care he took in the accurate presentation of costumes and customs, and an incredibly conscientious use of "Olde Englishe" language.

Clemens doth protest too much. Despite all the appurtenances [aspects] of the historical novel and Clemens's strenuous assertions of historicity, what has to be remembered is that *The Prince and the Pauper* is not folklore but—to use the most accurate term—fakelore. Like *Tarzan of the Apes*, Clemens's novel offers an Invented Past, Faux History.

A NATIONAL ANXIETY

The Prince and the Pauper, *Tarzan*, and *Fauntleroy*, then, may be regarded as "manuals of republicanism" because of their political critique and American advocacy of natural nobility. But in their compromised version of natural nobility and in their anxieties about succession, they reveal another side to this American sense of self-identity: a country that has made its forceful break with European parents now worries about being bereft, disowned, disinherited. The need to make ancestral assertions, in other words, the need to create Impostrous Pasts, reflects the subsequent anxieties of a country self-defined, parentless, Adamic, and ahistorical. Clemens's own response to his boyish fear of becoming an orphan took shape in a "historical" novel that likewise answered a national need for fictions of legitimacy.

The Doubles-Story in Crisis

Bruce Michelson

In the following viewpoint Bruce Michelson, of the University of Illinois English Department, says it is likely that in writing *The Prince and the Pauper*, Mark Twain was motivated by the popularity, literary respectability, and financial rewards of historically-based romances of the day. However, he maintains the novel has definite peculiarities which distinguish it from the popular "doubles-stories" of the time—in such stories in which two characters physically or psychologically mirror each other. Michelson says Twain presents strange psychological twists around the conventional narrative form of the historical romance, which have a peculiar effect, akin to later absurdist dramas. While critics like John Stahl and Jerry Griswold stress the themes of connection and identity formation in *The Prince and the Pauper*, Michelson says it is more about disintegration and loss of identity, and sees parallels with Czech novelist Franz Kafka's "The Metamorphosis." This is a horrifying story of a man who wakes up one morning to find he has been transformed into a giant insect and has disturbing themes of disconnection, isolation, and alienation. Michelson concludes that in *The Prince and the Pauper*, Mark Twain's reflections on the nature of the self, as neither real nor illusory, represented a psychological crisis which found further expression in *A Connecticut Yankee*.

In popular fiction . . . of the nineteenth century, one home-ground of the Anglo-American romantic novel remained the England of the Middle Ages and the Tudors. In Mark Twain's own heyday, the prose fiction that he found so damnably and enviably popular, and to his own temperament inescapably seductive, clanked about in chain mail, brandished broadswords, and fainted in furbelows [restrictive petticoats]. Charles Reade was a leader in a buzz of such novelists, and in the 1880s Reade was making a fortune. Given Mark Twain's competitive instincts and his drive to get rich, it is no surprise that from the start of that decade, in the canon of the great American realist, we find a good deal of romantic costume-drama, some of which, including *A Connecticut Yankee* and the completed version of *Number 44, The Mysterious Stranger*, figure regularly in theoretical discussion of Mark Twain's work; others, like *The Prince and the Pauper, A Personal History of Joan of Arc*, and *1601*, readers have often preferred to pass by.

CRITICAL RESPONSE IS DISMISSIVE

Judging by the response of Mark Twain's best critics, *The Prince and the Pauper* is an embarrassingly "well-made" tale, in a Victorian-drama sense of the phrase. Not only a romance by common definition, it is also a doubles-story, and in literary criticism doubles-stories have been talked almost to extinction, thanks to the installation of [the psychoanalytic interpretations by] Freud and Lacan in college English departments. Tales of this shape supposedly suggest anxieties about the id, the unconscious self, the repressed alternative personality whispering or howling for escape, and about public and private lives, bifurcated sexuality and gender confusion. Insofar as Mark Twain's critics have countenanced *The Prince and the Pauper*, they have sometimes followed such lines of thought, and debated what this doubles-tale might say about Clemens's double-self—his private and public identities, or the lingering poor boy within the great writer and the erstwhile tycoon. Nonetheless, those who doubt such dimensions in a tale for children have well-marked alternatives. Since disinherited princes and knights, changelings in royal cradles and nurseries, high-born souls traveling perilous roads incognito, fiancées in the thrall of usurpers, and miraculous rescues from mortal trouble are the stock-in-trade of historical melodrama, it seems fair to hold that Mark Twain as an author-entrepreneur was trying his hand at doing what Reade did, and Lew Wallace, Sardou, Victor Hugo, and others who had won not just riches but delirious praise from a worldwide public, praise such as Mark Twain had not heard (at least before *Huckleberry Finn*) for any work of his own.

As another subscription-trade entertainment, *The Prince and the Pauper* disappoints critics who for good reason decline to see more in it, or make more of it. Even so, its cultural staying-power is unquestionably high, as witnessed by the dramatizations, live-action films, animated features, and

THE MYSTERY OF MARK TWAIN

In the following afterword to a version of The Prince and the Pauper, *Everett Emerson commented on the issue of identity crises.*

The most important theme of *The Prince and the Pauper* is one the author would return to often: the mystery of identity. . . . The author's own life experiences brought him to his theme. . . . After Clemens met Olivia Langdon, he was eager to adopt genteel manners, and he can be said to have met the challenge with great success. But there is evidence that his transformation came at a price. In his last years Mark Twain began an unfinished novel called *Indiantown* that suggested his discomfort with his metamorphosis from Western humorist to Eastern gentleman. Here he describes one David Gridley, whose wife, Susan, has converted him into an "elaborate sham," a replacement for the man she married: "As far as his outside was concerned she made a masterwork of it that would have deceived the elect." "The real David, the inside David, the hidden David, was of an incurably low tone, and wedded to low ideals; the outside David, Susan Gridley's David, the sham David, was of a lofty tone, with ideals which the angels in heaven might envy." Significantly, David's wife [like Olivia Clemens] "edited David's letters for him, but not by request."

Perhaps the most subtle aspect of the treatment of identity in *The Prince and the Pauper* is the demand of three central characters to be recognized for who they are. The prince and the pauper both plead for recognition, and so does Miles Hendon. The reader can see in their protests a reflection of the author's desire to have his true literary identity recognized. The problem was that "Mark Twain" remained a mystery, even to the writer himself. On his deathbed, we are told by his biographer Albert Bigelow Paine—who was there—he talked about "Dual Personality, and discussed various instances that flitted through his mind—Jekyll and Hyde phases in literature and in fact." *The Prince and the Pauper* is a significant demonstration of the author's vital theme.

Everett Emerson, afterword in *The Prince and the Pauper*. New York: Oxford University Press, 1996.

picture-book versions this supposedly feeble story continues to inspire. As some species of entertainment the novel unquestionably works, and perhaps works too well to make trouble-loving professional readers happy. We run a risk of probing too deep when looking into such a book for hints about Mark Twain's mind, or the yearnings of an American public that self-evidently likes this book enough to make it a standard. The question is modest, yet stubborn: Is there anything really special about *The Prince and the Pauper*, other than its coming from Mark Twain's hand?

Much of the romantic appeal of doubleness has to do with worlds within, psychological or moral possibilities that, but for some fluke, might go undiscovered, unnamed, or forever restricted. In a good nineteenth-century Anglo-American doubles-story, whether it be [Poe's] "William Wilson" or [Stevenson's] *The Strange Case of Doctor Jekyll and Mr. Hyde*, [Conrad's] "The Secret Sharer" or [James's] "The Jolly Corner," the wastrel, killer, mutineer, or rampaging hedonist can be found out and at least for awhile released into the open air. And though the ending of such a tale might aspire to tragedy, one consoling implication can linger: that the self is possibly bigger than it seems, perhaps wilder and more terrible, but admirable in at least its dimensions and consequences. A grim prospect, however, that keeps cropping up in late-century variations, by authors like Conrad, Wilde, James, and Stevenson, is that the self is *not* transcendent but only dangerously malleable, down to the core, transformed and victimized by fate, peculiar chemicals or dark magic; and that identity might be manufactured by such things, by social forces and external influence.

So *The Prince and the Pauper* is one such late-century story about doubles and mistaken identities, and therefore one of an unevenly distinguished group of Anglo-American fictions (more American, this obsession, than Anglo). But if the book has distinguished kin, so what? The critical talk about *Prince* has often been hesitant, even dismissive. The consensus seems to be that this is a slick children's story, a potboiler of the stock well-made sort, with little to distinguish itself except some inert foreshadowings of interests that intensified later in Mark Twain's career: the injustices of the English monarchy, the miseries of the poor, the callousness and corruption of the titled classes, and perhaps the storytelling possibilities of setting resourceful boys adrift

with dim prospects, many enemies, and one true and mis-
valued friend.

A Tale About Unraveling

But *The Prince and the Pauper* does have peculiarities; it is a
double-story of a different hue, even amid the variety that
flourished in Mark Twain's prime. And a bit like *Huckleberry
Finn*, Mark Twain's romance of Tudor England does remain
at odds with stage and screen versions that have helped bring
the story back to popularity repeatedly in the past century. Indeed, this novel is less a novel of education than it is a tale of
self-loss and vanishing, in some ways more suggestive of
Kafka's "The Metamorphosis" than of *Oliver Twist, David Cop-
perfield*, or other tales in which boys wander London streets,
seeing and feeling the injustice of the commonfolk world, and
thereby learning to be humble and good. Though we can see
elements of that schooling in the tale of the displaced young
King Edward, they must contend with a great deal of narrative
interest in *non*being, in coming untethered from the clothes,
context, and ceremony that make kings and knights and poor
boys what they are. Though the tale attends more to King Edward's vagabonding than to Tom Canty's masquerade as a
prince and a monarch, the parallel tales, as far as they are so,
are not just about coming away from home and being mistaken for someone else, but also about coming apart.

Main Characters Are Orphans

Like Tom and Huck, Tom Canty is essentially fatherless;
John Canty, his biological sire, enters Tom's life only now
and then as a menace and a usurper, having bludgeoned to
death an impoverished old priest called Father William, who
has taught Tom a smattering of reading and Latin and
Greek, along with a few rudimentary courtesies and a touch
of compassion, and has been the best "father" Tom has
known. As for the other boy, with his mother long dead, Edward's closest ally and confidant in the palace is the Earl of
Hertford. Canty has no family; Prince Edward has no parents; the ragged knight Miles Hendon has spent years in a
foreign dungeon, not knowing that his own father and
mother have died in his absence.

Orphaning the three major characters seems more than a
gambit for keeping the plot lean and uncomplicated. The ex-
hilaration of the tale has to do with new identity and new

life. Tom accepts the chance wholeheartedly when it comes to him, and he is nearly destroyed by taking it, reaching a psychological abyss in the hour before he is rescued from the coronation, really the obliteration of himself by the acquired identity of Prince Edward. For his own part, Edward resists his new life at every turn, and because he does so he too is constantly in danger, from John Canty, from tramps and ruffians and the people they rob, from angry housewives, a justice of the peace and officers of the law, and most gravely from a mad hermit, who alone among the folk Edward meets in his adventures, actually believes that the young king is exactly who he says he is—and intends therefore to slaughter Edward as the heir of the villainous Henry VIII, despoiler of the Holy Catholic Church.

IDENTITY CRISIS

This moment of Edward's near-immolation is a tableau, paused over voyeuristically by the narrative. Bound, gagged, and writhing on a bed, the rightful king of England whimpers as the crazed hermit raves and gloats, this hermit who thinks that he is "naught but an archangel—I that should have been Pope!" Murder is interrupted by the arrival outside of Miles Hendon, who by the laws of romance seems the correct rescuer. Yet deceived by the hermit, Hendon rides away again, leaving Edward to be saved by the worst possible savior, John Canty, who thinks he is rescuing his own son Tom. So for a moment we have an inside-out Sacrifice of Isaac. A man-child, bound hand and foot, is posed tableau-fashion with an old man with a dagger and murderous intent; but the old man and sacrificer is the angel this time, and the rescuer is the father, who is nonetheless doubly *not* the father. For not only has John Canty mistaken Edward for a mad Tom; he has killed the Tom's good surrogate father, the priest who taught the real Tom the values Tom eventually needs to be a good king—meaning a good impostor king—a better king than the real king would have been if he had not lost his identity and his home, and gone wandering about as—well, not Tom, but nobody.

Am I making the moment stranger than it really is? Possibly. But judgment of that has to be grounded in a sense of whole novel's convolutions, and of its disruptions about this matter of who is really who. In Tom Stoppard's absurdist anti-drama *Rosencrantz and Guildenstern are Dead,* Rosencrantz (or maybe Guildenstern, for these wanderers too are so much "doubles" that they aren't quite sure themselves which one is which) asks the passing Player King, master of the wandering troupe headed for Elsinore, "What exactly do you *do?*" This is the answer:

> We keep to our usual stuff, more or less, only inside out. We do on stage the things that are supposed to happen off. Which is a kind of integrity, if you look on every exit being an entrance somewhere else.

INSIDE-OUT PLOT

Riddling, in a play full of riddles that cannot quite be worked out, which may be the point (if there can be a point) to a drama that subverts customary and complacently accepted distinctions between drama and real life, and assumptions that everything on the stage or off can be forced to make sense. But if the Player King's answer is not a good answer, it catches at least one good question. When dramatic or literary artifice commingles with life, or with history, or with values that thoughtfully or otherwise we like to call realistic, what then is the mix, the result? A fanatic about history, especially English and European history, to the extent that he fiddled for years with perfecting a History Game (a cumbersome ancestor of Trivial Pursuit) and railed at romantic and sentimental writers for playing loose with historical fact, Mark Twain in *The Prince and the Pauper* makes an actual king into the central character in a very tall tale, and swaps him off the throne in favor of an impostor, who is an unwilling, unwitting player-king. The real king—"real" in the sense of being an undisputed figure from history—becomes in the streets of London an unwilling impostor himself, a poor boy named Tom Canty, except that he doesn't accept the name, the identity, or the social station, and proclaims to almost everyone that he is Prince of Wales, and later that he is the rightful King Edward VI. And so the historical Edward becomes not merely a mystery boy but a lunatic; whether they "know" him as Tom Canty or not, everyone, including his guardian Miles Hendon (who eventually discovers that he is no longer himself—but more about that later), thinks that the king is mad. Back in the palace, everyone assumes that Tom Canty is Edward the Prince or Edward the King, but a prince or a king who has lost his wits, a mad boy on the English throne. In fact (if one can possibly get away with such a phrase) the one man in the world who believes that Edward, the "real" Edward, is indeed himself or at least what he says he is, believes himself an avenging archangel and tries to slaughter Edward for being King Edward. *The Prince and the Pauper* keeps to the usual stuff, more or less—only inside out.

Tom Stoppard did not write *The Prince and the Pauper.* In several ways, however, this children's story, whose simple, strong premise has fostered its translation or mistranslation to screen and picture-book, turns loops that take it out into a deep left-field of doubles-stories, where wide-wandering and exoticness are the norm. On one level the novel is manufactured history, loaded with quotations from real historians and upholstered with detail to give it a feel of authenticity but also of heightened fraudulence. That is a familiar and small paradox. These made-up adventures of actual historical figures, and these words conjured for them to speak, are familiar literary license; Shakespeare, Scott, and Browning, who all on occasion do the same thing, provide reassuring company, though Mark Twain's posturing elsewhere as champion of uncosmetized historical truth sets him a little apart, and makes this venture an anomaly. But within the large and rather commonplace paradox of romance-realism and make-believe history, there are others that though smaller in scope, do tighter, more surprising tumbles in the mind.

CONVOLUTIONS OF TOM AND EDWARD'S STORIES

For instance: though Tom and Prince Edward, thanks to a joke that goes too far, are mistaken not merely for each other but for each other as mad, the psychological experience sketched in for each boy, in his new and frightening circumstances, is absolutely opposite, and with opposite ramifications. Though the main attention of the narrative is on Edward-as-mad-Tom, it is Tom who undergoes, or at least begins to, a Shakespearean tragic transformation, while Edward's misadventures make him a shadow version of a tragic hero, or one of Shakespeare's less interesting classical-model protagonists. Tom veers toward a complete self-loss, or self-reinvention, into the public role that fate has handed him. By the end of the story, Tom is becoming a King Edward in truth, not only fancying and embellishing the opulence and pomp of the life that has snared him, but ultimately denying his own real mother on the streets of London as he makes his way to the Westminster coronation—which is to say, to his petrifaction into the identity of King. Edward therefore saves Tom's life in the halls of Westminster Abbey, saves him from becoming another stone effigy like those in the aisles all around the coronation throne, or another suit of empty armor like the one in which Edward has hidden the Great Seal of England: a rigid, hollow self that history, custom, and brutal necessity have contrived.

Edward's danger is Tom's inside out. Because he knows perfectly well—dangerously well—who he is, Edward is constantly in trouble with people who don't believe him and also from people who do. The moral lessons of ordinary life he learns only with peril and suffering, and his one genuine ally accepts and defends Edward as a "king of shadows and dreams," not quite mad, yet not genuine either, a creature in some zone between fraudulence, delusion, and honest truth. So Edward, like some preteen Cato or Coriolanus, is nearly destroyed because he will not change; and for his part Tom is nearly undone because deep within he veers close to changing absolutely.

MILES HENDON'S LOSS OF IDENTITY

I referred to Miles Hendon, the ragged knight who befriends the dethroned Edward, as having some part in fostering the Tom Stoppard funhouse-qualities of this book, as another nonperson in a bewildering array. Hendon himself has been disinherited while fighting overseas and languishing in a foreign dungeon, yet Hendon is not a refurbished Ivanhoe. Miles Hendon is rather Ivanhoe turned inside-out. In Scott's romance, having been disowned by his father Cedric, Ivanhoe returns from the Crusades in disguise, first as a palmer, then as an unknown knight with "Desdichado" (wretched one) inscribed on his shield, a faceless suit of armor within which rides a willful man. Hendon comes home to his estate as himself, and is denied to be himself: by his own brother Hugo, by his fiancée Lady Edith to whom Hugo is now married, and by the remaining servants of the house, Miles's father and mother having died in his absence. All of that would imply that Hendon's brother and bride are denying themselves as well, or some great part of their own identity.

BRIDGE AS A SYMBOL OF BEING NOWHERE

It turns out that Edith is lying both as the former beloved and as the happy wife, having been forced to marry Hugo and hating him thoroughly. So Miles, having returned home as himself, finds that he is now nobody, and is jailed with Edward for impersonating himself; or, rather, both of them are jailed as a pair, a player-king and a player-knight. In *The Prince and the Pauper* there is no dignity to disinheritance, and no plausible recourse. There is no joust, no romantic identity as the boy or man of mystery. Hendon recovers himself by a fluke: going to the palace on a whim, he is discovered accidentally by the whipping-boy who has heard of Hendon from the rediscovered king, and Edward back on his throne restores Hendon's lands, lady, and title by royal decree. It matters that when Edward first meets Hendon, the just returned knight is living in rooms on London Bridge, a place between places. It also matters that one of the tour de force passages in the novel, a passage in which Mark Twain's gusto as a writer seems to reach a peak, is about this somewhere that is nowhere, a centuries-old nontown of perpetual transition, where people live and die without going anywhere, or really being anywhere, and feel endangered by the prospect of stable dry earth and identity:

> The Bridge was a sort of town to itself; it had its inn, its beer houses, its bakeries, its haberdasheries, its food markets, its manufacturing industries, and even its church. It looked upon the two neighbors which it linked together,—London and Southwark—as being well enough, as suburbs, but not otherwise particularly important. It was a close corporation, so to speak; it was a narrow town, of a single street a fifth of a mile long, its population was but a village population, and everybody in it knew all his fellow townsmen intimately, and had known their fathers and mothers before them—and all their little family affairs into the bargain. It had its aristocracy, of course—its fine old families of butchers, and bakers, and what-not, who had occupied the same old premises for five or six hundred years, and knew the great history of the Bridge from beginning to end, and all its strange legends; and who always talked bridgy talk, and thought bridgy thoughts, and lied in a long, level, direct, substantial bridgy way. It was just the sort of population to be narrow and ignorant and self-conceited. Children were born on the Bridge, were reared there, grew to old age and finally died without ever having set a foot on any part of the world but London Bridge alone. Such people would naturally imagine that the mighty and interminable procession which moved through its street night and day, with its confused roar of shouts and cries, its neighings and bellowings and bleatings and its muffled thunder-tramp, was the one great thing in this world, and themselves somehow the proprietors of it. And so they were, in effect—at least

they could exhibit it from their windows, and did—for a consideration—whenever a returning king or hero gave it a fleet-
ing splendor, for there was no place like it for affording a
long, straight, uninterrupted view of marching columns.

Men born and reared upon the Bridge found life unendurably
dull and inane, elsewhere. History tells of one of these who
left the Bridge at the age of seventy-one and retired to the
country. But he could only fret and toss in his bed; he could
not go to sleep, the deep stillness was so painful, so awful, so
oppressive. When he was worn out with it, at last, he fled
back to his old home, a lean and haggard spectre, and fell
peacefully to rest and pleasant dreams under the lulling mu-
sic of the lashing waters and the boom and crash and thun-
der of London Bridge.

Overblown though this might be, it is certainly the cadenza
passage of *The Prince and the Pauper*, a celebration and a
shiver about a historical place and a dreamed condition of
perpetual nonarrival, a life literally on the road. The oddness
in the prose is symptomatic of Mark Twain's narrative style
throughout the novel, a style genteel and Anglo-mannered,
sometimes well past the point of affectedness. . . . It seems a
plausible guess that as a stylistic outing, *The Prince and the
Pauper* was at least partially an I-can-do-it-too demonstration
for the sake of literary respectability, proof that this popular
Missouri-Washoe-pilot-journalist-comedian could lay on the
stylistic sauce just like the revered romancers on the Anglo-
American scene—meaning those British writers whose
names were being intoned in American schoolrooms. Yet imitation, even for show or monetary advantage, can have other
sides and motives, just as a put-on can mean not only mockery but obliteration of the mocker. And aside from proving, or
rather showing off, a knowledge of broader lexicons and
sidelights of English history and everyday life, this "long,
level, direct, substantial bridgy" lie that Mark Twain tells may
signify what the Bridge itself seems to mean for Miles Hendon and the displaced Prince Edward.

TWAIN'S PSYCHOLOGICAL AND LITERARY CRISIS

The Prince and the Pauper may be about many things that
critics have sometimes grudgingly conceded it might be
about: the plight of the poor, the need of lawmakers to feel
the edge and bite of law, the need of the highborn and comfortable to understand the suffering all around them, and to

apprehend the "there but for fortune" condition that many of us are in on this earth. But this book is also about limbo, about how easily the self can slip away, or be obliterated precisely because it will *not* slip, about the perils of being incompletely made, and of being made too solidly and well. And if any of this rings true, then one extractable theme of the novel might be that there is no extractable theme, because the self is mystery, neither illusory nor real, just as the "real" and historical people in the novel are neither fact nor illusion. At the same mirror, in the same moment, a real prince and a dreamed-up boy can stand together and admire what they see in the glass, because each of them is "truly" like the other, history-book true, and yet a shadow of a dream. The first of two Old England novels that Mark Twain published in his lifetime, *The Prince and the Pauper* ransacks the trick-bag of romance while raising a fuss against the mode. Though injustice, squalor, ignorance, and degrading social habit move through the foreground—as satire, at least in part, of the popular-fiction taste for glorious, tidy days of yore—the plot of the novel owes nearly everything to the sort of romantic story structure that was selling so well, and that Mark Twain liked railing against. In that simple way, the story of Tom and Edward is a prelude to *A Connecticut Yankee in King Arthur's Court*, for that ambivalent quarrel with romance radiates with higher intensity in the tale of Hank Morgan and the Lost Land. But this inchoate [undeveloped] question about selfhood also prowls there, in the later work, and as a heightened presence. After *Huckleberry Finn*, Mark Twain's meditations on the contingency of selfhood, and on the contingency of literary modes, grow both surer, more complex, and more self-aware, and in *Yankee* the literary and psychological crises achieve connections that are unprecedented in Mark Twain's fiction.

CHRONOLOGY

1835
On November 30 Samuel Langhorne Clemens is born to John M. and Jane L. Clemens in Florida, Missouri; Andrew Jackson is president; Halley's comet is visible in the sky; Alexis de Tocqueville's famous study of the new American nation, *Democracy in America*, is published and predicts the coming of a distinctive American literature.

1837
John Clemens becomes a county judge; Victoria is crowned queen of England; Charles Dickens's *Oliver Twist* is published.

1838
The Underground Railroad, which helps slaves escape to the North, is established; the transatlantic steamship service begins.

1839
The Clemens family moves to Hannibal, Missouri, on the Mississippi River; the abolitionists form a national party.

1843
Young Sam Clemens spends the first of five consecutive summers on the Quarles family farm near Florida, Missouri; large-scale westward migration begins in the United States.

1844
Clemens contracts measles by climbing into Will Bowen's sickbed during the epidemic; Samuel Morse sends the first telegraphic message.

1846
The Clemens family sells household furniture to raise money; the United States declares war on Mexico.

1847
John Clemens dies; Samuel Clemens works for the *Hannibal Gazette;* Thomas Edison and Jesse James are born.

1848

Clemens becomes an apprentice for the *Missouri Courier;* California gold rush begins; political and social revolutions sweep Europe.

1850

Clemens's brother Orion begins publishing the *Hannibal Western Union;* California becomes a state.

1851

Clemens begins working for his brother Orion as a printer.

1852

On July 4 Frederick Douglass says blacks should not celebrate Independence Day since so many of them are slaves; Harriet Beecher Stowe's *Uncle Tom's Cabin* is published.

1853

Clemens leaves Hannibal to work as a printer in St. Louis, New York, and Philadelphia.

1854

Abraham Lincoln calls for the gradual emancipation of slaves; the Republican Party is formed.

1856

Clemens's first published letter, signed Thomas Jefferson Snodgrass, appears in the *Iowa Daily Post.*

1857

Clemens is an apprentice riverboat pilot and lives on the Mississippi River.

1858

The steamboat *Pennsylvania* explodes, killing Clemens's brother Henry; Theodore Roosevelt is born; Charles Darwin's *Origin of the Species* is published.

1860

Lincoln is elected president.

1861

Clemens's piloting career ends when the Civil War stops river traffic; he campaigns with the Confederate irregulars around Marion County; he travels with brother Orion to Nevada and fails at prospecting for silver.

1862

Clemens is a reporter and writer for the *Territorial Enterprise* in Virginia City.

1863

Lincoln signs the Emancipation Proclamation in January; on February 3 Clemens first uses the Mark Twain byline; Thackeray dies.

1864

Twain leaves Virginia City for San Francisco; he works for the *San Francisco Morning Call.*

1865

In March Lincoln is sworn in for a second term as president; on April 9 the Civil War ends.

1866

Twain sails to Hawaii, then New York, and conducts his first lecture tour in San Francisco.

1867

The Celebrated Jumping Frog of Calaveras County and Other Sketches is published; Twain sails as a travel correspondent for the San Francisco *Alta California* aboard the *Quaker City* to the Mediterranean (this becomes the basis for *The Innocents Abroad*); Karl Marx's *Das Kapital* is published.

1868

Twain courts Olivia "Livy" Langdon and becomes secretly engaged to her; Twain meets Harriet Beecher Stowe and Joseph Twichell.

1869

Twain publishes *The Innocents Abroad;* W.E.H. Lecky's *A History of European Morals* is published.

1870

Twain marries Langdon at Elmira; their first child, Langdon Clemens, is born prematurely; Dickens dies.

1871

Twain rents a house in Hartford's Nook Farm.

1872

Roughing It is published; Susy Clemens is born; Langdon Clemens dies; Twain goes to England alone and lectures in London.

1873

Twain signs a deed on a Nook Farm area property; he joins Hartford's Monday Evening Club; Twain goes to England with his family; he writes *The Gilded Age* with Charles Dudley Warner.

1874

Twain begins writing *Tom Sawyer;* his daughter Clara is born.

1876

The Adventures of Tom Sawyer is published; Twain begins *The Adventures of Huckleberry Finn* and research for *The Prince and the Pauper;* Alexander Graham Bell achieves the first electronic transmission of the human voice.

1877

Twain outlines *The Prince and the Pauper;* Twain gives the infamous Whittier birthday celebration speech.

1878

Twain sails for Europe with his family.

1880

Twain and his family live in Hartford; Jean Clemens is born; Twain writes *The Prince and the Pauper; A Tramp Abroad* is published; Twain invests in the Paige typesetting machine.

1881

The Prince and the Pauper is published.

1885

The Adventures of Huckleberry Finn is published.

1886

R.L. Stevenson's *Dr. Jekyll and Mr. Hyde* is published.

1889

A Connecticut Yankee in King Arthur's Court is published.

1890

The Man That Corrupted Hadleyburg is published; the stage adaptation of *The Prince and the Pauper* opens in New York.

1891

Twain and his family end their period of residence in Hartford and go to Europe.

1893

A stock market crash in June leads to a national financial panic and what is called the worst depression in U.S. history.

1894

Tom Sawyer Abroad is published; with the failure of his publishing company, Twain is bankrupt.

1895

Twain begins a worldwide lecture tour to pay off his debts.

1896

The Personal Recollections of Joan of Arc is published; Susy Clemens dies in Hartford; Harriet Beecher Stowe dies.

1898

Twain and his family live in Vienna, where he meets Sigmund Freud; in winning the Spanish American War, America establishes itself as a world power.

1900

Twain meets W.E.H. Lecky; he introduces Winston Churchill on his first American lecture tour.

1901

Twain lives in New York; Livy is very ill; Theodore Roosevelt becomes president.

1904

Livy dies; Clara has a nervous breakdown; Jean has epileptic seizures; the Russo-Japanese War begins.

1905

Twain celebrates his seventieth birthday with a banquet at the White House.

1906

What Is Man? is published without author identification; A.B. Paine joins the household to write Twain's biography.

1907

Twain undertakes his last transatlantic trip to England; he receives an honorary degree from Oxford University.

1909

Jean Clemens dies; Clara Clemens marries and moves to Europe.

1910

On April 19 Halley's comet is again visible in the night sky; two days later, on April 21, Mark Twain dies.

FOR FURTHER RESEARCH

BIOGRAPHIES

Susy Clemens, *Papa: An Intimate Biography of Mark Twain*. Ed. Charles Neider. New York: Doubleday, 1985.

Everett Emerson, *Mark Twain: A Literary Life*. Philadelphia: University of Pennsylvania Press, 2000.

William Dean Howells, *My Mark Twain: Reminiscences and Criticism*. New York: Harper and Brothers, 1910.

Justin Kaplan, *Mark Twain and His World*. New York: Simon and Schuster, 1974.

John Lauber, *The Making of Mark Twain*. New York: American Heritage, 1985.

Milton Meltzer, *Mark Twain Himself*. New York: Wings Books, 1960.

A.B. Paine, *Mark Twain: A Biography. The Personal and Literary Life of Samuel Langhorne Clemens*. 3 vols. New York: Harper and Brothers, 1912.

Henry Nash Smith, *Mark Twain: The Development of a Writer*. Cambridge, MA: Harvard University Press, 1962.

Edward Wagenknecht, *Mark Twain: The Man and His Work*. New Haven, CT: Yale University Press, 1935.

REFERENCE

J.R. Le Master and James D. Wilson, eds., *Mark Twain Encyclopedia*. New York: Garland, 1993.

R. Kent Rasmussen, *Mark Twain A to Z: The Essential Reference to His Life and Writings*. New York: Oxford University Press, 1996.

ANALYSIS AND CRITICISM

Frank Baldanza, *Mark Twain: An Introduction and Interpretation*. New York: Holt, Rinehart, and Winston, 1961.

198   *Readings on* The Prince and the Pauper

Van Wyck Brooks, *The Ordeal of Mark Twain.* New York: Dutton, 1920.

Peter Brunette, "Faces in the Mirror: Twain's Pauper, Warner's Prince," in *The Classic American Novel.* Eds. Gerald Peary and Roger Shatzkin. New York: Frederick Ungar, 1977.

Louis J. Budd, *Critical Essays on Mark Twain, 1910–1980.* Boston: G.K. Hall, 1983.

———, *Mark Twain: The Contemporary Reviews.* New York: Cambridge University Press, 1999.

Bernard DeVoto, *Mark Twain's America.* Boston: Little, Brown, 1932.

Helen E. Ellis, "Mark Twain: The Influence of Europe," *Mark Twain Journal,* Winter 1968.

Everett Emerson, afterword to *The Prince and the Pauper,* by Mark Twain. New York: Oxford University Press, 1996.

Victor Fischer, foreword to *The Prince and the Pauper,* by Mark Twain. Berkeley and Los Angeles: University of California Press, 1983.

Robert Gale, "*The Prince and the Pauper* and *King Lear,*" *Mark Twain Journal,* Spring 1963.

John C. Gerber, *Mark Twain.* Boston: Twayne, 1988.

Robert Giddings, *Mark Twain: A Sumptuous Variety.* Totowa, NJ: Vision, 1985.

Michael Patrick Hearne, "Mark Twain, 1835–1910," in *Writers for Children.* Ed. Jane Bingham. New York: Charles Scribner's Sons, 1988.

Lawrence Howe, *Mark Twain and the Novel: The Double Cross of Authority.* New York: Cambridge University Press, 1998.

Katie de Koster, ed., *Readings on Mark Twain.* San Diego: Greenhaven, 1996.

Lucy Rollins, introduction to *The Prince and the Pauper,* by Mark Twain. New York: Oxford University Press, 1996.

Lin Salamo, introduction to *The Prince and the Pauper,* by Mark Twain. Eds. Victor Fischer and Lin Salamo. Berkeley and Los Angeles: University of California Press, 1979

David E.E. Sloane, "Humor and Social Criticism: *The Gilded Age* and *The Prince and the Pauper,*" in *Mark Twain as a Literary Comedian.* Baton Rouge: Louisiana State University Press, 1979.

WORKS BY MARK TWAIN

The Celebrated Jumping Frog of Calaveras County and Other Sketches (1867)

The Innocents Abroad, or The New Pilgrims' Progress (1869)

Mark Twain's (Burlesque) Autobiography and First Romance (1871)

Roughing It (1872)

The Gilded Age: A Tale of Today (with Charles Dudley Warner) (1873)

Mark Twain's Sketches (1874)

Sketches Old and New (1875)

The Adventures of Tom Sawyer (1876)

Ah Sin (with Bret Harte) (1877)

Punch, Brothers, Punch! and Other Sketches (1877)

A True Story of the Recent Carnival of Crime (The Facts Concerning the Recent Carnival of Crime in Connecticut) (1877)

"1601" or Conversation at the Social Fireside as It Was in the Time of the Tudors (1880)

A Tramp Abroad (1880)

The Prince and the Pauper (1881)

The Stolen White Elephant, Etc. (1882)

Life on the Mississippi (1883)

Adventures of Huckleberry Finn (1885)

A Connecticut Yankee in King Arthur's Court (1889)

The Man That Corrupted Hadleyburg (1890)

The American Claimant (1892)

Merry Tales (1892)

The $1,000,000 Bank-Note and Other New Stories (1893)

Tom Sawyer Abroad (1894)

The Tragedy of Pudd'nhead Wilson and the Comedy of Those Extraordinary Twins (1894)

The Personal Recollections of Joan of Arc (1896)

Tom Sawyer Abroad, Tom Sawyer Detective, and Other Stories (1896)

Following the Equator (1897)

How to Tell a Story and Other Essays (1897)

*The Man That Corrupted Hadleyburg and Other Stories and
   Essays* (1900)
To the Person Sitting in Darkness (1901)
A Double Barreled Detective Story (1902)
*The Jumping Frog in English, Then in French, Then Clawed
   Back into Civilized Language Once More by Patient
   Unremunerated Toil* (1903)
My Debut as a Literary Person with Other Essays and Stories
   (1903)
Extracts from *Adam's Diary* (translated from the original
   manuscript) (1904)
A Dog's Tale (1904)
Editorial Wild Oats (1905)
King Leopold's Soliloquy: A Defense of His Congo Rule
   (1905)
Eve's Diary (translated from the original manuscript)
   (1906)
The $30,000 Bequest and Other Stories (1906)
What Is Man? (1906)
Christian Science (1907)
A Horse's Tale (1907)
Extract from *Captain Stormfield's Visit to Heaven* (1909)
Is Shakespeare Dead? From My Autobiography (1909)

PUBLISHED POSTHUMOUSLY

Mark Twain's Speeches, compiled by F.A. Nast; introduction
   by W.D. Howells (1910)
Death Disk (1915)
The Mysterious Stranger (1916)
Mark Twain's Letters, edited by Albert Bigelow Paine (1917)
Who Was Sarah Findlay? (with a suggested solution of the
   mystery by J.M. Barrie) (1917)
*The Curious Republic of Gondour and Other Whimsical
   Sketches* (by Samuel Clemens) (1919)
The Writings of Mark Twain, thirty-seven volumes, edited
   by Albert Bigelow Paine (1922–1925)
The Adventures of Thomas Jefferson Snodgrass, edited by
   Charles Honce (1928)
Mark Twain's Notebook, edited by Albert Bigelow Paine
   (1935)
*Mark Twain in Eruption: Hitherto Unpublished Pages About
   Men and Events,* edited by Bernard DeVoto (1940)
The Love Letters of Mark Twain, edited by Dixon Wecter
   (1949)
Mark Twain to Mrs Fairbanks, edited by Dixon Wecter
   (1949)
The Autobiography of Mark Twain, edited by Charles
   Neider (1959)

Mark Twain–Howell Letters: The Correspondence of Samuel L. Clemens and William Dean Howells, 1872–1910, two volumes, edited by Henry Nash Smith and William M. Gibson (1960)

Mark Twain's Letters to Mary, edited by Lewis Leary (1961)

Letters from the Earth, edited by Bernard DeVoto (1962)

The Outrageous Mark Twain: Some Lesser-Known but Extraordinary Works, with "Reflections on Religion" Now in Book Form for the First Time, edited by Charles Neider (1987)

Mark Twain: Collected Tales, Sketches, Speeches, and Essays, two volumes, edited by Louis J. Budd (1992)

Mark Twain: Historical Romances, edited by Susan K. Harris (1994)

Tales, Speeches, Essays, and Sketches, edited by Tom Quirk (1994)

The Oxford Mark Twain, edited by Shelley Fisher Fishkin (1996)

When in Doubt, Tell the Truth, and Other Quotations from Mark Twain, edited by Brian Collins (1996)

INDEX

death penalty, 108, 109
DeVoto, Bernard, 25, 34, 63, 127, 157
  Twain's personal papers compiled
    by, 62
Dickens, Charles, 10, 35, 81, 84, 184
  and international copyright
    protection, 82
  use of humor by, 80
Dickinson, Leon T., 69
Dr. Jekyll and Mr. Hyde
  (Stevenson), 83, 183
Durkheim, Emil, 165

Emerson, Everett, 19, 21, 33, 182
  on Clemens's determinism, 23
  on Clemens's social aspirations,
    28
  on literary character "the
    Unreliable," 25
Emerson, Ralph Waldo, 8
England
  Twain's attitude toward, 77-78,
    82, 157, 161-62
  changes in, 79-80
  see also setting, historical
English Rogue, The (Head and
  Kirkman), 70-71
Enterprise (Nevada newspaper), 10,
  26, 27, 98
Errol, Cedric, 177

Fairbanks, A.W., 135
Fairbanks, Mrs. Mary Mason, 29,
  58-61
Faulkner, William, 110
Foner, Philip S., 136
Frohman, Daniel, 56
Fulton, Joe, 12

"Gallant Fireman, A," 19-20
Gilded Age, The (Warner and
  Twain), 30, 72, 124, 146
Goodman, Joseph T., 10, 25, 63, 64,
  98
Gould, Jay, 76
Great War Syndicate, The
  (Stockton), 83
Griswold, Jerry, 172

Haggard, Rider, 83
Halley's comet, 13, 32
Handlin, Oscar, 167
Hannibal Courier (newspaper), 19
Hannibal, Missouri, 15-17, 20, 24
Hannibal Western Union
  (newspaper), 19, 20
Harper's (magazine), 75, 86, 90
Harte, Bret, 59, 81, 140

Hartford, Connecticut, 33, 62, 63, 66
  and influence of, on Twain's
    writing, 65, 67, 74-75
  residents of, included other
    writers, 73-74
Hawaii, 27, 28
Hayes, Rutherford, 147
Head, Richard, 70
Henry Esmond (Thackeray), 81
Henry IV (Shakespeare), 96
*History of European Morals from
  Augustus to Charlemagne* (Lecky),
  148, 150
Hooker, John, 59
Howe, Lawrence, 11
Howells, William Dean, 79, 86, 150,
  163
  as advocate of good breeding, 58
  and avoidance of soldiering, 24
  and complaint about literature of
    his time, 83
  and confidence about reception of
    Prince and the Pauper, 135
  Connecticut Yankee reviewed by,
    76, 147
  Innocents Abroad reviewed by, 30
  on plot of *Prince and Pauper*,
    87-88, 104
  and praise for seriousness of
    Prince and Pauper, 90, 142
  and suggestions for changes to,
    61
  on Twain's character portrayal in
    Prince and Pauper, 89
  Twain's letters to, 53, 84, 108, 153
    concerning plot of *Prince and
      Pauper*, 131
    on inconsistency of human
      beings, 129
    indicating author's perception of
      Prince and Pauper as serious
      work, 141
  on vulgarity of humorists, 80
*Huckleberry Finn, The Adventures
  of*, 30, 65, 97, 138, 178
  acknowledged as finest work, 10,
    31, 73
  controversies over, as school text,
    11
  critical of society, 133
  delay in completion of, 134, 140
  era of American history recorded
    by, 162
  negative reactions of critics to, 66,
    90, 91, 131
  originally intended for
    publication with *Prince and
    Pauper*, 55

206   *Readings on* The Prince and the Pauper